Hobart's Best
Bush, Coast & City Walks

By
Ingrid Roberts

Woodslane Press Pty Ltd
10 Apollo St
Warriewood, NSW 2102
Australia
Email: info@woodslane.com.au
Tel: (02) 8445 2300   www.woodslane.com.au

First published in Australia in 2011 by Woodslane Press, reprinted with corrections 2019

Copyright © 2011 Woodslane Press Pty Ltd; text and photographs © 2011 Ingrid Roberts

All rights reserved. Apart from any fair dealing for the purposes of study, research or review, as permitted under Australian copyright law, no part of this publication may be reproduced, distributed, or transmitted in any other form or by any means, including photocopying, recording, or other electronic or mechanical methods, without the prior written permission of the publisher. For permission requests, write to the publisher, addressed "Attention: Permissions Coordinator", at the address above. Every effort has been made to obtain permissions relating to information reproduced in this publication. The information in this publication is based upon the current state of commercial and industry practice and the general circumstances as at the date of publication. No person shall rely on any of the contents of this publication and the publisher and the author expressly exclude all liability for direct and indirect loss suffered by any person resulting in any way from the use or reliance on this publication or any part of it. Any opinions and advice are offered solely in pursuance of the author's and publisher's intention to provide information, and have not been specifically sought.

National Library of Australia Cataloguing-in-Publication entry

Author	Roberts, Ingrid.
Title:	Hobart's best bush, coast & city walks : the full-colour guide to over 38 fantastic walks / Ingrid Roberts.
ISBN:	9781921683664 (pbk.)
Notes:	Includes bibliographical references and index.
Subjects:	Trails--Tasmania—Hobart—Guidebooks. Nature trails--Tasmania--Hobart--Guidebooks. Walking--Tasmania—Hobart--Guidebooks. Hobart (Tas—Description and travel—Guidebooks.
Dewey Number:	919.461

Printed in Australia
Designed by Coral Lee and Jenny Cowan

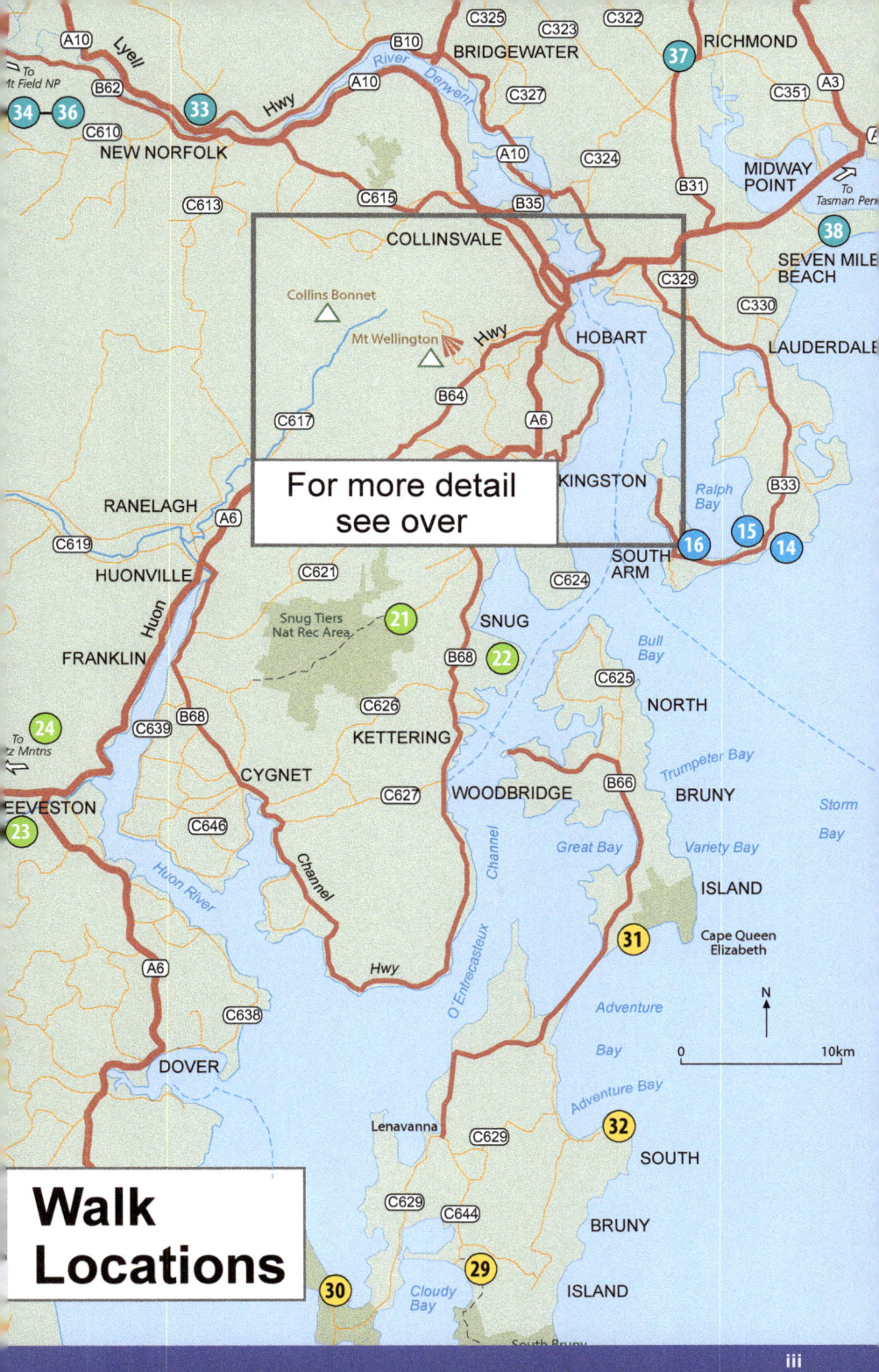

Walk Locations

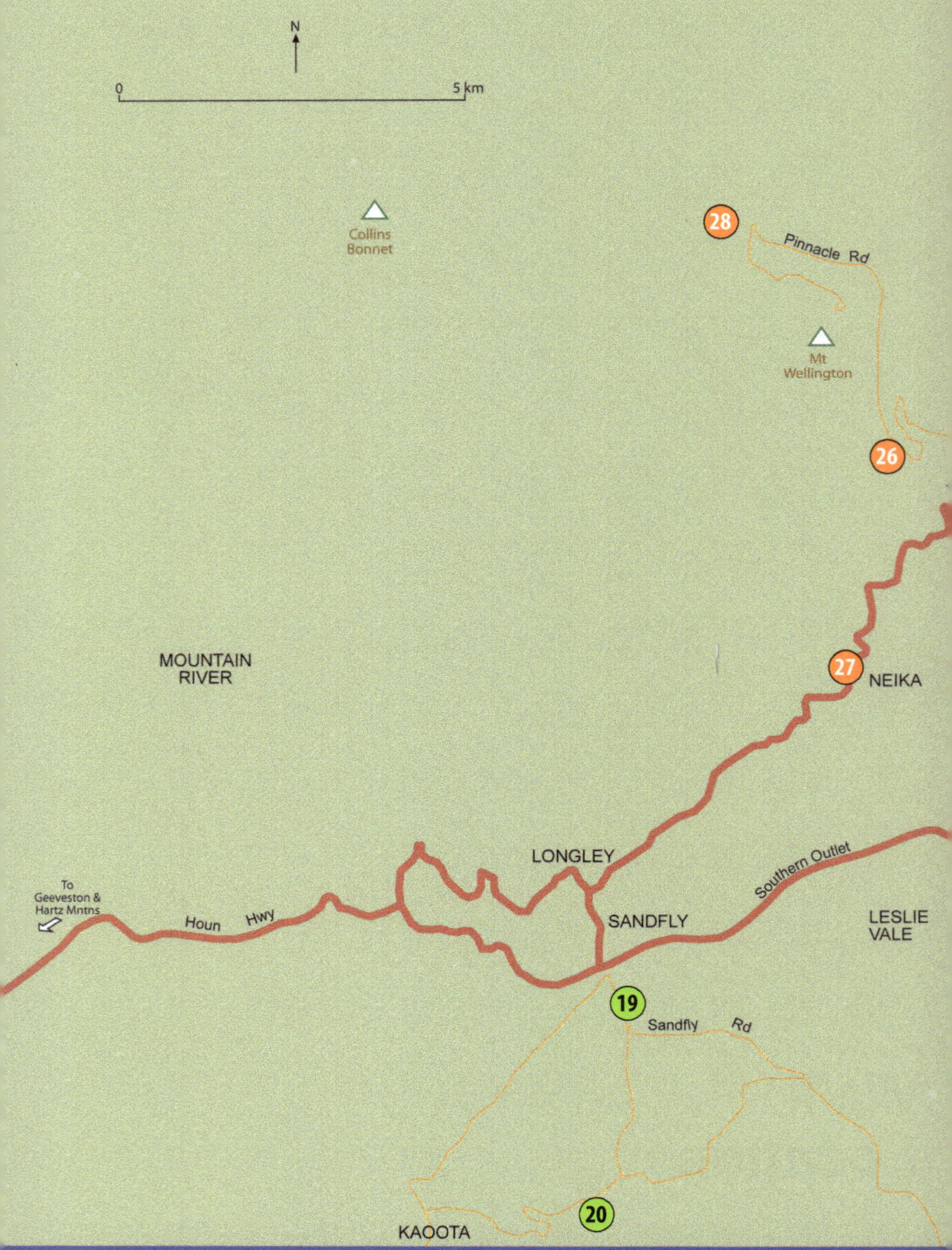

Contents

Regional location maps .... iii-v

Introduction 1

    Being prepared 5

Walks at a glance 6

Hobart's Best Bush, Coast & City Walks

    Central Hobart 11

    Eastern Shore and South Arm Peninsula 51

    South of Hobart 91

    The "Mountain" 127

    Bruny Island 151

    Further afield 175

Safety 206

Further reading 209

Index 210

About the author and acknowledgements 213

Other books from Woodslane Press 214

Introduction

Hobart is nestled on the River Derwent, in between the Wellington Range to the west and the Meehan Range to the east. The modern city is divided by the river, which follows a deep crack in the earth's crust that was created through tectonic and volcanic activity which began after Jurassic times. The city was the first British colonial penal settlement on the island (initially at Risdon Cove, but moved after a year in 1804 to Sullivan's Cove), established at least in part to discourage French interest in the island. The new population of convicts, guards and other immigrants eventually displaced the area's long-established indigenous *Mouheneener* people.

Part of the attraction of the area to the British was the number of local watercourses that originate about halfway up Mt Wellington – they indeed proved vital during the early days of the settlement. They have also played a great part in shaping the land, cutting steep gullies and forming bays and headlands where they meet the river.

One of the best ways to explore this city and its environs, with its rich history and relaxed lifestyle, is on foot. This guide will lead you along hidden creeks and interesting coastlines, through dense bushland and historic suburbs, and along the way you will spot small treasures of geology, flora and fauna, some of which are unique to Tasmania. Above all I hope you will enjoy the wide views and the friendly people to be met along the tracks.

Some of the walks in this guide lead you along or through the sandstone layers that remain under the dolerite cliffs so distinctive of much of Tasmania. On other walks you will be able to admire the dolerite itself or climb to the top of it. Where magma outpourings reached the surface it formed basalt, as can be seen at Cornelian Bay (walk 3).

Hobart has a number of bushwalking groups that cater for young and old. If you enjoy walking in a larger group and want to tap into their vast amount of local knowledge, contact them and join the one that suits you best. Useful information about bushwalking and groups can be found at www.bushwalkingaustralia.org.au.

Introduction

Public Transport

The *At a glance* section at the beginning of each walk contains information about how to reach the start of the walk by car and, if possible, by bus. Please double-check bus route numbers or obtain more detailed information from the Metro Hotline T 132201, www.metrotas.com.au, or visit the Metro shop next to the GPO in Hobart.

Walk grades and times

All the walks are graded for their difficulty, and include an estimate of the time needed to complete them. Grading is generally based on the most difficult segment(s) of the walk, so in some cases you may be able to skip a more difficult segment if you prefer an easier walk. Providing you are healthy (check this with your doctor if you are new to walking), you need not be discouraged by steep hills or longer climbs. Just remember that we all puff when we go uphill; having to lift our own weight is not easy for anyone. Reduce your speed to allow your body to get used to the idea and plod on. You may surprise yourself by how far you get. Generally start off with the easy, short walks and work up to the longer, harder ones. Note that poor weather conditions can make even easy walks more hazardous, for instance by causing tracks to become slippery.

Easy – Clearly marked tracks; some short steep gradients or sets of steps; few if any natural obstacles. Generally suitable for children but see under *Walking with children* below: supervision is of course essential in areas where there are unfenced cliff tops, busy roads to cross or watercourses.

Medium - Suitable for people of average fitness; marked tracks or routes, some of which may be overgrown. Longer steep gradients and natural obstacles such as fallen logs and rocks.

Hard – Suitable for experienced and fit walkers; marked tracks or routes sometimes rough or overgrown, or wet with steep gradients and natural obstacles such as rocks and fallen logs; good preparation and navigational skills essential.

Introduction

Walking times

These have been calculated using a rule developed by William Naismith (founding member of Scottish mountaineering club) and modified to Australian conditions. While this rule allows for track condition, climbs and ascents, it assumes that you are an adult of average fitness carrying a medium weight backpack and you are not stopping anywhere. In reality, you may be keen to stop and admire natural wonders that you encounter along the way, take lots of photos, have curious toddlers or dogs in tow or just like to stop for a rest frequently. Also, the larger your walking party the longer your walking time is likely to be. No rule exists to allow for these extras that really make walking so worthwhile, so the times should simply be seen as a approximate indication, they are not designed to create a challenge! Always err on the side of caution when estimating grades and times for yourself - it is better to have a little extra time on hand than to run into the dark or miss arranged transport or important appointments.

Walking with children

While many of the walks in *Hobart's Best Bush, Coast and City Walks* are suitable for children, only a parent can judge what their child can manage.

Some walks lead along unfenced cliff-tops or watercourses or require a road crossing. This is where parental supervision is essential. A ratio of one adult per child is ideal, but with older children you can probably get away with one adult to two children. Very young children are often more capable of walking than one would think; they complain of tiredness but really mean they are a bit overawed – and bored - by the wide open spaces. Providing them with short term goals such as reaching a certain feature, giving them things to look for and periodically resting to hand out 'go food' will reassure them.

Taking your dog

As a rule dogs are not allowed in National Parks, whereas reserves and other public spaces generally require you to walk dogs on a leash. Always adhere to local signage. Suitable walks for your four-legged friend are indicated in the following introductory *Walks at a glance* section.

Introduction

Track closures

Tracks can be closed or rerouted for a variety of unforeseeable reasons such as flooding, bushfires, fallen trees or unstable ground. Closure can also be due to track development and maintenance. For information on this, contact the relevant authority: either the Parks and Wildlife Service, T 6233 6560, www.parks.tas.gov.au, or the local council of the area.

Looking after the environment

Leaflets on minimal impact bushwalking are available from the Parks and Wildlife Service but in short:

- **Take your rubbish out with you**
- **Stay on tracks**
- **Don't pick wildflowers**
- **Don't interfere with wildlife**
- **Respect historical and cultural sites**
- **Do not light fires** (Tasmanian plants, such as gum trees and the leaf litter beneath them, contain highly flammable oils that will ignite readily with just one spark, particularly on hot windy days in summer, and turn into a wildfire in minutes. If you are a smoker, please put out your cigarette butt very carefully indeed)

Please help to prevent the spread of the terrible root-rot fungus ***Phytophthora cinnamomi*** by removing any soil (the carrier of this disease) from your gear, especially your boots, as frequently as possible, but particularly when asked by signage and at the end of every walk.

A whisper on toileting

The best option is to try to ensure you'll need no more than a wee for the duration! Use toilets where they are provided. If you must go during a walk make sure you are well off the track (hang something brightly coloured on a tree to find your way back to the main track) and away from water courses. Bury faeces and toilet paper to a depth of at least a good hand span. The aim is to reach the root zones of plants, where it will act as compost. It is also important to note that no bush area is remote enough for someone not to stumble upon tissue or toilet paper left on the surface by another and be offended by it. It is possible for women to drip dry and not need a tissue. An increasing number of people want to enjoy our beautiful natural environment - and not see it spoilt by unsightly and unhygienic bits of paper.

Being prepared

A very old Tasmanian joke runs "if you don't like the weather – come back in half an hour". Bear this in mind when you set off on a walk: snowfalls have been recorded on Mt Wellington, even in summer! **Weather** changes occur rapidly and often without warning, especially at higher altitudes. The happy Hobartian walker wears non-cotton trousers (cotton is just awful when it gets wet) and carries a set of thermals, warm gloves, a beanie, a sun hat, a warm jacket and a raincoat in their backpack all year round. This allows them to feel smug when the weather changes.

Your **feet** deserve to be looked after; after all they do a lot of work. For all of the walks in this book graded easy/medium you are advised to wear strong, comfortable walking shoes or trainers, with a good grip, that have been 'run in'. For the harder walks half boots or full walking boots are essential. Wear soft socks to prevent blisters and carry band-aids to cover blisters as soon as you notice them. Keep toenails trimmed.

It is wise to carry plenty of **drinking water**, for hot days at least one litre per person for every two hours of walking. A flask of hot water and separately tea, coffee, cocoa or soup powder (according to your taste) can also be a real life saver. Always carry some **nibbles** in the form of mixed nuts, dried fruit, seeds and chocolate or jelly beans for those moments when walking power fades, particularly with children, but also as emergency food. Carry both water and nibbles where they are readily accessible to prevent that 'Oh, I will put off drinking because I can't be bothered to stop' scenario - which will get you dehydrated in no time. For longer walks don't forget to take plenty of food.

Walk with at least one **companion** if out in the bush and away from urban areas and let someone know where you are going and when you expect to return. **EPIRBs** and satellite phones can be hired from the Parks and Wildlife Service.

For notes on walking safety see page 206.

There seem to be a lot of rules about bushwalking, but when you think about them you will see that most of them come under the umbrella of 'common sense' and are quite easy to make into a habit. They are there to help everyone to enjoy the wonderful experience of exploring new tracks in a 'cared-for environment'.

So go out and have fun!

Walks at a glance

	Walk	Page	Distance (km)	Time
Central Hobart				
1	Hobart Waterfront and Battery Point	12	6.5 circuit	2 hrs
2	Queen's Domain and Botanical Gardens	18	4.5 circuit	2 hrs
3	Cornelian Bay	24	5.7 circuit	1½ hrs
4	Knocklofty Reserve	28	5.2 circuit	2 hrs
5	Cascade Brewery, Gardens and Hobart Rivulet	32	4.4 return	1¾ hrs
6	Mt Nelson Signal Station and Truganini Reserve	36	4.9 one way	2¾ hrs
7	Alexandra Battery and Lower Sandy Bay	42	3 circuit	1 hrs
8	Waterworks and Pipeline Track	46	4.6 one way	1¼ hrs
Eastern Shore & South Arm Peninsula				
9	Shag Bay	52	4.8 return	1½ hrs
10	Lindisfarne Bay and Gordons Hill	56	6.8 circuit	2¼ hrs
11	Rosny Hill Lookout and Foreshore	62	4.2 circuit	1.2 hrs
12	Rosny to Bellerive Beach	66	8.3 circuit	2½ hrs
13	Waverley Flora Park	72	2.9 circuit	1¼ hrs
14	Calverts Lagoon, Goat Bluff & Calverts Beach	76	5.5 circuit	1½ hrs
15	Tangara Trail and Gorringes Beach	81	5.9 circuit	1¾ hrs
16	Arm End	86	7.25 circuit	2 hrs
South of Hobart				
17	Kingston Beach to Boronia Beach	92	3.3 return	1¼ hrs
18	Fossil Cove and Tinderbox Hills	96	4.6 return	2 hrs
19	North West Bay river	100	1.6 return	40 mins
20	Kaoota Tramway Track	104	12 return	3 hrs
21	Snug Falls	108	2.1 return	50 mins

Walks at a glance

Grade	Public transport	Café	Dogs	Highlights
Easy/med	-	Yes	Yes	History, views, gardens
Easy/med	-	Yes	Yes*	History, views, bush, gardens
Easy	Yes	Yes	Yes*	Cemetery, beach, boat sheds
Easy/med	Yes	-	Yes	Bush and wildflowers, frogponds, views
Easy	Yes	-	Yes	History, old brewery, gardens, public art
Med/hard	Yes	Yes	Yes*	Bush, views, history, bus ride
Easy	Yes	Yes	Yes	History, lighthouse, beach, play area
Med/hard	Yes	Yes	-	History, water storage dams, bus ride
Easy/med	Yes	-	Yes	Water views, history, bush, botanical
Easy/med	Yes	-	Yes	Water views, history, bush, lookout
Easy/med	Yes	-	Yes	Water views, lookout
Medium	Yes	Yes	Yes	Water views, lookouts, history, beach
Easy/med	Yes	-	Yes	Botanical, lookouts, history
Easy/med	Yes	-	-	Birdlife, lookout, history, beach
Easy/med	Yes	-	Yes	Bush, wildflowers, birdlife, water views
Easy/med	Yes	Yes	Yes	Water views, birdlife, history
Easy	Yes	Yes	Yes*	Beaches, water views, sandstone cliffs
Easy	-	-	Yes	Rock arch, water views, forest
Easy	-	-	-	Boulder stream, dolerite cliffs, forest
Easy	-	-	Yes	History, views, bush
Easy/med	-	-	Yes*	Forest, waterfall

Walks at a glance

Walk	Page	Distance (km)	Time
South of Hobart (continued)			
22 Conningham Reserve	111	7.7 circuit	2½ hrs
23 Kermandie Falls	116	5 return	2 hrs
24 Hartz Peak	120	12.5 return	4½ hrs
"The Mountain"			
25 Fern Tree, Silver Falls and Dunns Creek	128	2.8 circuit	1¼ hrs
26 Zig Zag Track, Summit and Icehouses	134	7 circuit	4 hrs
27 St Crispins Well	140	10.5 return	3 hrs
28 Collins Bonnet	144	14 return	6½ hrs
Bruny Island			
29 East Cloudy Head	152	13 return	4½ hrs
30 Labillardiere Peninsula - Luggaboine	158	5 circuit	1½ hrs
31 Cape Queen Elizabeth	162	12 return	3½ hrs
32 Fluted Cape	168	5.4 circuit	2½ hrs
Further afield			
33 New Norfolk	176	5.9 circuit	2 hrs
34 Lake Dobson and Pandani Grove	182	2.2 return	50 mins
35 Tarn Shelf	186	14 circuit	5½ hrs
36 Lake Nicholls	192	4 return	1¾ hrs
37 Historic Richmond	196	2.5 circuit	50 mins
38 Devils Kitchen to Waterfall Bluff	200	6.7 return	3¼ hrs

* strictly on-leash

Walks at a glance

Grade	Public transport	Café	Dogs	Highlights
Easy/med	-	-	Yes*	Caves, cliffs, beaches, fish farm
Med	-	-	Yes*	Forest, waterfall
Hard	-	-	-	Mountain views, glacial features, alpine vegetation
Easy/med	Yes	Yes	-	Wet forest, ferny gullies, waterfall, history
Med/hard	-	-	-	Mountain views, alpine vegetation, history
Easy	-	-	-	Views, forest, history
Hard	-	-	-	Mountain views, subalpine vegetation
Medium	-	-	-	Beach, coastal cliffs, views, wildlife
Easy	-	-	-	Coastal views, beaches
Medium	-	-	-	Coastal cliffs, siltstone formations, beaches, rookery
Med/hard	-	-	-	Sea Cliffs, views, wildlife, forest
Easy	Yes	Yes	Yes	River views, history, autumn colours
Easy	-	-	-	Lake, sub-alpine vegetation, glacial feature
Hard	-	-	-	Glacial features, tarns, alpine vegetation, autumn colours
Medium	-	-	-	Forest, lake
Easy	Yes	Yes	Yes	History, river, art and crafts
Easy/med	-	-	-	Coastal features, sea cliffs, waterfalls, forest

Central Hobart

When Hobart was first settled in 1804, Lieutenant-Colonel David Collins selected Sullivans Cove for his settlement party to disembark because of its deep harbour and the source of good running water, the Hobart Rivulet.

Industries such as whaling and shipbuilding sustained the young settlement and it is still possible to walk around Hobart and imagine those early days. The scenery has not changed significantly and many of the old buildings remain, sometimes modified to suit modern demands and lifestyles. Compared to other Australian capitals Hobart is small and walking is a fine way to get around. Busy city streets and natural bushland are in close proximity to each other and it is easy to experience both in as little as a couple of hours walking.

The walks in this chapter will allow you to explore Hobart's waterfront, its oldest suburb, historic signal station and battery, bushland and the all important source of water.

North Hobart and Tasman Bridge

1 Hobart Waterfront and Battery Point

Hobart has one of the best deepwater ports in the world. Its waterfront is lined with historic sandstone buildings that were once warehouses and factories, but which now contain art galleries, shops, eateries and offices. A set of sandstone steps leads from Salamanca Place, on the southern side of the waterfront, up to Battery Point. This, one of Australia's oldest suburbs, was in days gone by the home of mariners who worked out of the port.

This walk, which is interpreted with signage along the way, is an invitation to explore the rich history of this area.

At a glance

Grade: Easy/medium
Time: 2 hrs, but allow at least 2½ hrs
Distance: 6.5 km circuit
Conditions: Some short, steep sections and a set of steps; dogs on a leash
More info: www.hobartcity.com.au, www.narryna.com.au, www.maritimetas.org, Salamanca Markets every Saturday 0830-1500

Getting there
Car: From the Tasman Highway leading into the city turn left at the signposted *Domain Sportscentre* and *Cenotaph* turn-off; turn right into the car park (free 3 hr parking)

Hobart waterfront

1 Hobart Waterfront and Battery Point

Walk directions

1 Start at the *Walk/Cycle* sign near the entrance to the car park. Leaving the Cenotaph to your left, continue along the highway past Hobart's old Cement Works and the Tudor style institute building for the Royal Engineers on your left. Soon after the highway becomes Davey Street turn left into Hunter Street. Interpretive signage, telling the story of Hunter Island, can be found on the corner of Davey and Hunter Streets and a number of bronze markers in the pavement indicate the former coastline before Hunter Island was artificially joined to the waterfront. Walk as far as the University of Tasmania/School of Art, which has retained the character of the old IXL Jam Factory that was operating here until the 1960s.

Salamanca Market

2 Turn right (leaving Macquarie Wharf and a large Quarantine shed to your left) into Franklin Wharf and cross the swing bridge. To your left you will see Stephen Walker's bronze sculptures commemorating the Antarctic explorer Bernacchi and on your right Victoria Dock with some of Tasmania's fishing fleet. The next dock on your right is the famous Constitution Dock with the historic Customs House in the background.

This is where the Sydney to Hobart Yacht Race contestants moor after the race. As you proceed towards the dock's entrance and across the old lifting bridge you will also pass an old steam crane- an old port railway siding line is still visible in the pavement here. Continue to follow the waterfront past Elizabeth Street Pier and the Ferry Wharf until you reach a set of traffic lights. Across the wharf is the dock of the *Aurora Australis*, Australia's Antarctic flagship. Cross the traffic lights at the junction of Murray Street, Morrison Street and Castray Esplanade toward the entrance of Parliament House Lawns, a leafy expanse of lawns and gardens in front of the Tasmanian House of Parliament (a popular site for community events, protests and media interviews). Walk through this park's central pathway to the opposite end, which leads onto Salamanca Place, home of the colourful and very popular Saturday markets.

1 Hobart Waterfront and Battery Point

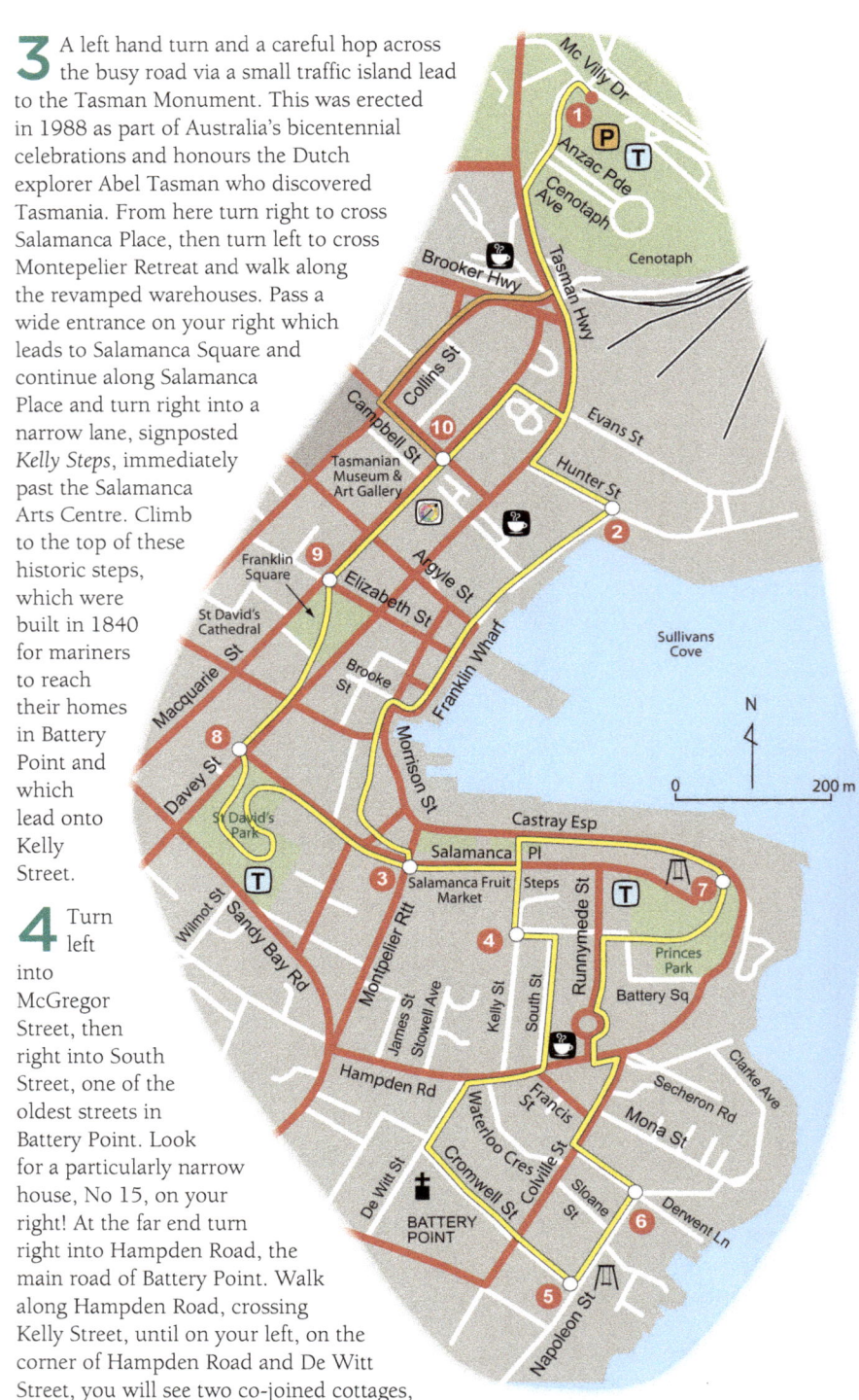

3 A left hand turn and a careful hop across the busy road via a small traffic island lead to the Tasman Monument. This was erected in 1988 as part of Australia's bicentennial celebrations and honours the Dutch explorer Abel Tasman who discovered Tasmania. From here turn right to cross Salamanca Place, then turn left to cross Montepelier Retreat and walk along the revamped warehouses. Pass a wide entrance on your right which leads to Salamanca Square and continue along Salamanca Place and turn right into a narrow lane, signposted *Kelly Steps*, immediately past the Salamanca Arts Centre. Climb to the top of these historic steps, which were built in 1840 for mariners to reach their homes in Battery Point and which lead onto Kelly Street.

4 Turn left into McGregor Street, then right into South Street, one of the oldest streets in Battery Point. Look for a particularly narrow house, No 15, on your right! At the far end turn right into Hampden Road, the main road of Battery Point. Walk along Hampden Road, crossing Kelly Street, until on your left, on the corner of Hampden Road and De Witt Street, you will see two co-joined cottages,

1 Hobart Waterfront and Battery Point

Arthurs Circus

one with a modern tin roof the other with its original shingle roof. (A side trip to 'Narryna Heritage Museum' is possible from here by continuing along Hampden Road to No 103 – see box below.) Turn left into De Witt Street and left again into Cromwell Street where you will find cottages made from handmade bricks that are laid in a distinctive old pattern. St Georges Church next door, built in 1838, is a landmark that was once used by visiting sailors. At the far end of Cromwell Street turn left into Napoleon Street.

5 Cross Napoleon Street to visit a small playground and park that overlooks Hobart's old ship building yards in which convict labourers were once employed. The distinctive round tower of Australia's first casino, Wrest Point, is also visible from here. Follow Napoleon Street to its junction with Trumpeter Street.

6 On this corner are some fine examples of working men's brick cottages built in 1858. Turn left into Trumpeter Street and then right into Colville Street. Cross the road towards a stone garden wall, behind which is an overgrown garden and, set well back from the street, a well hidden stately home that was built in 1840 for Charles McLachlan, the Governor of the Bank of Van Diemen's Land. At the end of Colville Street turn left back into Hampden Road and soon afterwards right into Runnymede Street. Walk through the well

Out and about – Narryna Heritage Museum

This museum, at 103 Hampden Road in Battery Point, is situated in the original homestead built for Captain Andrew Haig in 1836 and showcases the elegant lifestyle of a wealthy merchant and his family in Hobart during the earlier 1800s. The museum also houses one of the largest costume collections in the southern hemisphere. Admission: adults $6, concessions $5, families $15. Open weekdays 1030-1700, summer weekends 1230-1700 pm, winter weekends 1400-1700. Some holiday closures. T 6234 2791, www.narryna.com.au.

1 Hobart Waterfront and Battery Point

St David's Park

known quaint little circle of cottages known as Arthurs Circus, then continue along Runnymede Street. Turn right into McGregor Street and enter the top of Princes Park though a well-defined leafy gateway, then follow the wide footpath through the park's centre, a favourite lunchtime resting spot for many locals. Looking right through the mature, shady European trees you will be able to catch sight of the Derwent Estuary. Towards the lower end of the park you will find the old Signal Station which was first installed in 1812 to signal the arrival of ships in the River Derwent.

7 Exit the Park and turn left onto Castray Esplanade and left again to return to Salamanca Place. Follow the place to its full length this time - a small side trip around the perimeter of St David's Park (Hobart's first cemetery), on your left, is well worth the effort.

8 At the end of Salamanca Place, turn right into Davey Street. Cross over at the traffic lights at Murray Street and continue along Davey Street on the fenced footpath that leads into Franklin Square, fronted at the southern end by some historic government buildings. Walk diagonally

Out and about – The Tasmanian Maritime Museum

Situated in the historic Carnegie Building at the corner of Argyle and Davey Streets, this houses Tasmania's largest and most varied collection of maritime artefacts, including an aboriginal bark canoe, a fully equipped one third size replica of a 19th century whale boat, ship models and figure heads as well as a collection of 40,000 photographs and numerous paintings. Admission: adults $7, concessions $5, students (13-18 years, under 12s free) $4, families $16. Bookings taken for guided walks: $12, school groups $3 per student. Open daily 0900- 1700. Some holiday closures. T 6234 1427, www.maritimetas.org.

1 Hobart Waterfront and Battery Point

through the Square, past the fountain, towards the GPO Clock Tower (which can be seen through the trees). Exit Franklin Square at the corner of Macquarie and Elizabeth Streets.

9 Walk down Macquarie Street, past the grand historic sandstone buildings of the General Post Office to the left and the Hobart Town Hall to the right. (Another short side trip to the Tasmanian Maritime Museum can be taken from here by turning right into Argyle Street to find the museum on your right near the end of the block). Continue past the Tasmanian Museum and Art Gallery on your right and the old City Hall on your left.

10 Turn left into Campbell Street to walk along the side of the City Hall and then right into Collins Street. At the end of Collins Street you can see an interesting sculpture and some interpretation about the Hobart Rivulet and the problems that this low lying area had with flooding. Cross the Brooker Highway towards a set of concrete steps which lead up to the side of the newly built Baha'i centre for learning. Turn right to find the entrance to the café and the centre itself with its distinctive dome roof. It was designed to high standards of energy efficiency and water conservation. Open 0900 – 1700 weekdays, 1000 – 1500 Sat. closed Sunday. Exit the site via its front entrance towards a lone gum and a set of traffic lights. Cross the highway and turn left to retrace your steps to the start of the walk.

Old Signal Station

2 Queen's Domain and Royal Tasmanian Botanical Gardens

Queen Victoria gifted this area to the people of Hobart in 1860. It contains many public facilities such as the Royal Tasmanian Botanical Gardens, Government House, a range of sporting venues including the Hobart Aquatic Centre, as well as the historically important Gunpowder Magazine, Wireless Institute, Beaumaris Zoo site and the Soldiers Memorial Avenue. The area is also of importance for its natural heritage, particularly the remnant endemic grassland with its shallow dolerite soils. During this walk you will have the chance to see many of these interesting features.

At a glance

Grade: Easy/medium

Time: 1½ - 2 hrs plus time to visit the gardens

Distance: 4.5 km circuit

Ascent/descent: 90 m / 90 m

Conditions: Some short, steep sections and a set of steps; dogs on a leash

More info:
www.hobartcity.com.au,
www.soldierswalk.org.au,
www.rtbg.tas.gov.au

Getting there

Car: From Brooker Ave leading into the city turn left into the Domain Hwy (signposted *Royal Tasmanian Botanical Gardens*) then right into Lower Domain Rd and park in the semi-circle car park on your right

Gunpowder Magazine

2 Queen's Domain and Royal Tasmanian Botanical Gardens

Walk directions

1 The walk starts at the southeastern end of the car park. Head down the narrow path along a small gully wooded with She Oaks and Blackwoods with Bursaria and Kangaroo Grass in the understorey. Cross the gully via duck boarding near its top. Swing left to an interpretive shelter, with information on native grasslands and fauna, beside a bitumen road. The track continues on the other side of the road; follow it past the *Soldiers Memorial Avenue, Gunpowder Magazine, Hobart Cenotaph* sign and a sign listing the names of soldiers who gave their lives during WWI, until you reach a junction with the main Soldiers Walk.

2 Turn right into the Walk and climb the wooden steps leading up to the Soldiers Memorial Oval, then right again to skirt the oval to the small Soldiers Oval car park. Turn right and cross the Lower Domain Road to a small gravelled car park diagonally opposite. Locate a narrow foot track which runs parallel to the road and turn right passing below some large water tanks until, just after a blue water main signpost, you reach a post which is marked *Jogging Track*.

3 Turn left and follow the narrow, winding bushtrack which leads through She Oaks, Bursaria and Kangaroo Grass with the odd White Gum. Ignore a track leading off to the left after about 100 metres, and continue in a northerly direction. To your right you can enjoy views across the Derwent River towards the Meehan Range (note this area is crisscrossed with tracks, do not let them confuse you - basically you are heading to the top of the hill!). Cross a gravelled path and turn left at the next junction, only about 20 metres away. Keep walking north uphill until you see a car park and picnic area under

2 Queen's Domain and Royal Tasmanian Botanical Gardens

some tall mature White Gums. The road to the summit loops clockwise around the top of the hill.

4 The summit is a fine place to rest and perhaps enjoy a snack. It is the site of the historic wireless institute. It affords panoramic views: westwards to the Wellington Range and its foothills, to the north up the Derwent towards the Bowen Bridge, Cornelian Bay, Selfs Point and New Town Bay to the northeast, and across the Derwent to the prominent Mt Direction (part of the Meehan Range) and Hobart's Eastern Shore suburbs.

5 To continue the walk, find the *Queen's Domain Summit Lookout* sign and the summit car park, north of the cream, weatherboard wireless institute building. Take the faint track that leads from the western edge of the car park in a downhill direction through native grassland to a junction a short distance away, then turn left to follow the contour of the hill towards a small stand of She Oaks and a junction with a wider track. Turning left again, you will find that the track leads you back to the edge of the Summit Road. Along the way, looking right, there are views towards

Eastern Rosella

Out and about – Wireless Institute

This cream Federation-style weatherboard building was erected in 1912 to become Australia's second government owned coastal radio station. In those times it was considered an engineering feat as it was capable of regular contact, by Morse code, with Macquarie Island. Later it became part of a nationwide network of maritime and naval communications. Today it functions as the clubrooms of the Radio and Electronics Association of Southern Tasmania with meetings held every Wednesday from 1200-1600. Visitors are welcome.

2 Queen's Domain and Royal Tasmanian Botanical Gardens

Mt Wellington and the suburb of New Town. Walk along the track, parallel to the road until you come to a junction with a directional *Wireless Institute* sign on the left. Eastern Rosellas can be found here among the Tasmanian endemic Blue Gums. Turn right here and descend, spying the CBD on the way, to the bitumen crossroads a short distance away and a *Soldiers Memorial Oval* sign.

6 Carefully cross towards the upper oval and skirt around its top edge past an interpretive sign about the restoration work being undertaken in this area. When you reach another *Soldiers Memorial Oval* sign, turn left through a chainmesh gate towards a toilet block. Turn right and then left to reach the

Beaumaris Zoo art gate

2 Queen's Domain and Royal Tasmanian Botanical Gardens

top of the wooden steps you climbed on your way up earlier. Descend down the steps. (It is possible to shorten the walk here by retracing your steps to the car park).

7 Continue along the wide Soldiers Memorial Avenue until you reach a sign on the left to *Gunpowder Magazine*. Turn left then right to view the magazine, with its thick sandstone walling, and rejoin the avenue. Continue along the avenue past a park bench and an interpretive sign until you see a track leading off to the left just past a lone house. Turn left and walk around the front of the house to Carriage Drive. Cross it carefully towards a tall, painted picket fence which marks the boundary of the historic Beaumaris Zoo site, where the last captive Tasmanian Tiger died. Walk along the picket fence and turn left where it fronts onto the Lower Domain Road with a gravelled footpath. The zoo was relocated to this site in 1923 and closed in 1937. Remnants of a pool and animal enclosures can still be seen through the art gate (which carries more detailed information about the history of the zoo).

8 After you have passed the ornate entrance gate to Government House, cross to a footpath on the other side of the road. This path leads to the equally ornate main entrance to the Royal Tasmanian Botanical Gardens.

9 Here you have the option of visiting the Gardens or returning to the start of the walk by taking the steps to the left of the entrance gates which lead back onto the Lower Domain Road. Turn right and follow the Gardens boundary fence to the semi-circle car park taking care in the traffic, which can be quite heavy at times.

2 Queen's Domain and Royal Tasmanian Botanical Gardens

Out and about – Royal Tasmanian Botanical Gardens

Established in 1818, these are the second oldest botanical gardens in Australia. Features include a Tasmanian section (where plants have been grouped into habitats such as alpine, rainforest, dry sclerophyll etc), a refrigerated display of the flora of Macquarie Island in the sub-Antarctic plant house and a beautiful old conservatory as well as 'Pete's Vegie Patch' of ABC Television fame. The far eastern end of the gardens, through the old original brick enclosure, contains a beautiful Japanese garden with water features and a Huon Pine fountain. A restaurant, visitor centre and gift shop are situated near the original main entrance gates. Visitor maps are available via the internet or at the gardens. The Gardens are open every day during daylight hours.

3 Cornelian Bay

This bay was named for the small, semi-precious, dark red, siliceous carnelian stones that were found here and which had weathered out of a lava flow of bubbly basalt. Remnants of this flow can be found at the bay's northern end near sea level. Cornelian Bay Point, the headland above, was once a government farm that supplied vegetables and produce to the early settlers of Hobart Town. It is now a cemetery. The area below the cemetery is used as a dog exercise area. The southern end of the bay has a number of picturesque, historic boat sheds that are still in use. On the foreshore you can find picnic facilities with barbecues, a children's playground and a restaurant. This leisurely walk consists of two halves; a loop taking in the headland and cemetery to the north and a return walk through She Oak woodland along the foreshore starting above the boat sheds to the south.

At a glance

Grade: Easy

Time: 1½ hrs but allow at least 2 hrs

Distance: Total 5.7 km – Cemetery loop 1.7 km plus foreshore return 4 km

Conditions: Well-formed, wide tracks except for beach; partly shaded; any season

More info:
www.millingtons.com.au,
T 6278 1244 (current operator of cemetery)

Getting there

Car: From the Brooker Ave heading into the city, turn left at Risdon Rd then immediately right over bridge onto Queens Walk; turn right uphill, past a block of flats to Cornelian Bay; park at northern end of bay

Bus: Metro route 20, hourly, ask driver to stop

3 Cornelian Bay

Walk directions

1 From the car park turn left along the foreshore. If the tide is out you can make the small side trip along the beach to inspect the bubbly basalt rocks of relatively recent (tertiary, only two million years!) volcanic origin, but watch out - they are slippery! Turn back and enter the track near a large *Cornelian Bay Point* sign outlining that major re-development is planned for this area.

2 A wide gravelled path leads uphill from here, curving to the right around the edge of the bay as it rises above the fenced cliff edge. The track leads through remnant coastal vegetation of She Oaks, Black Wattle and Bursaria. Ignore a short track leading off to the left. Near the top, as the track begins to loop to the left onto a closed road, is an open grassy area with mature White Gums. A park bench invites you to enjoy the views southwards across the bay towards the Queen's Domain with the Royal Tasmanian Botanical Gardens and the dinosaur shape of the Tasman Bridge.

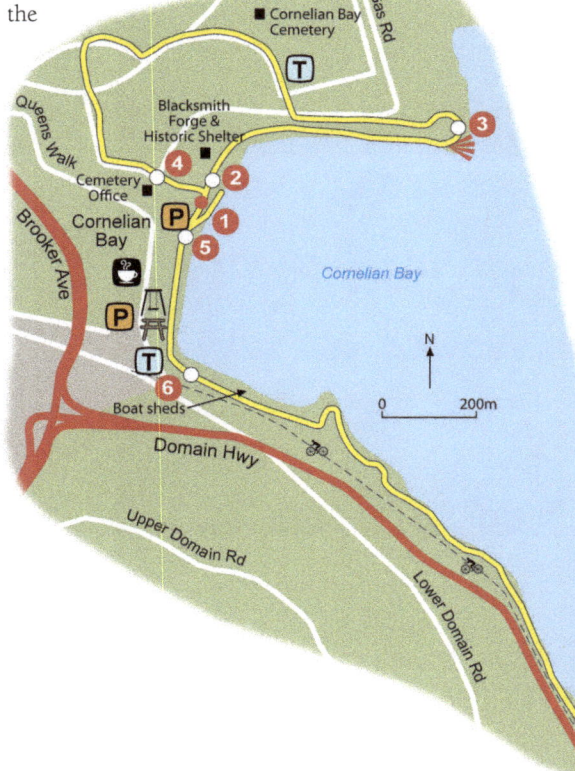

3 Follow the loop, which leads onto the closed sealed road, and walk along this until, after a short distance, you come to a wide weldmesh gate on your right which is on the boundary of the Cornelian Bay Cemetery. Enter through a narrow gate to the left of the wide gate, making sure you leave the gate as you find it. To your right is the lawn cemetery with a rose garden. This is a pleasant place

3 Cornelian Bay

to reflect and wander among the graves. Heading uphill towards the centre of the cemetery, you will find a water feature near some very old Macrocarpa Pines. From here you can see Selfs Point, with its oil refinery and fuel storage depot, and across the River Derwent the cliffs of the Bedlam Walls that are the edge of the fault that forms the river valley. Work your way back downhill towards the southwestern corner of the cemetery nearest Cornelian Bay and towards Mt Wellington, until you see a historic shelter.

4 The colonial architect Henry Hunter designed this shelter, erected in 1873. It is made of Huon Pine and has a copper roof. Nearby is a blacksmith's forge which was constructed out of sandstone in 1830. It was part of the former government farm buildings. The Cemetery Office is located in the original Jewish receiving house which was also designed by Hunter. It overlooks a modern day sports grounds, once lined with soldier's residences. Follow the main road,

Government Farm Blacksmith Shop

Walk variation

Instead of taking the foot track as described in point five above, you can walk along the cycle track which avoids crossing the railway line at the other end and therefore enables you to cross the Domain Highway and incorporate a visit to the magnificent Royal Tasmanian Botanical Gardens into your walk. For information on the Royal Tasmanian Botanical Gardens see Walk 2.

3 Cornelian Bay

which now swings to the left, leaving the homestead to your right and continue downhill toward the car park and starting point. A flock of Sulphur Crested Cockatoos can often be seen here.

5 For the second half of the walk head south along the beach, past a restaurant, playground, amenities block and picnic area, to its far end and walk up a foot track with some steps to a small parking area. Turn left and locate the start of the track which runs parallel and below a railway line and a cycle track and is marked by a sign.

6 A number of narrow foot tracks lead down to the boat sheds below, from where you can see across to Cornelian Bay Point. About 200 metres along the track some concrete steps with a handrail lead down to Pipeclay Point for another chance to view the bay and boatsheds. Walk the length of the track, which ends at a barrier and a notice advising that the track is closed from here due to an unsafe railway crossing beyond this point.

7 Return the way you came.

Hobart history - Cornelian Bay

Tasmanian Aboriginal people of the Mouheneenne band lived in this area for eight thousand years. Profiles of their shell middens can still be seen in the dark sands near the top of the low cliffs of Cornelian Point. After settlement in 1804 much of the area was a government farm which was subdivided and sold in 1860. By this time a new cemetery was needed for Hobart and after much deliberation Cornelian Bay was chosen. Convict labour was used to clear and fence the site which was opened in 1872. Twelve year-old Bridget Ryan was the first person to be buried in the new cemetery and her grave can still be seen. You can also find many historic gravestones of famous people such as those of Martin Cash, the bushranger, George Adams, founder of Tattersalls and Tenis Sterio, the king of the world's gypsy communities, who died in Hobart in 1943. Each religious denomination has a designated area. Other special sections include War Graves, the Garden of Remembrance and the Crematorium Gardens.

4 Knocklofty Reserve

The Knocklofty Summit Loop track has recently been upgraded, which makes this walk a very pleasant experience, suitable for families and dogs. The walk starts with an easy climb and then leads up around the southwestern, shady side of the hill, allowing views across to Mt Wellington. The track then curves east towards the summit of Knocklofty before zig-zagging down a newly constructed path which leads through light bush. There are patches of natural 'rock gardens' where many interesting understorey and rockery plants can be spotted and, of course, they form a wonderful habitat for birds and other animals such as Echidnas. Grassy areas near the top of the hill are home to the endangered Eastern Barred Bandicoot.

At a glance

Grade: Easy/medium
Time: 2 hrs
Distance: 5.2 km circuit
Ascent/descent: 200 m / 200 m
Conditions: Well marked track, gentle climb and descent, shady in places
More info: Hobart City Council, Parks & Customer Service Division, T 6238 2886, www.hobartcity.com.au; www.friendsofknocklofty.org

Getting there

Car: From the city drive up Liverpool St, go right into Molle St then left into Goulburn St and left again into Forest Rd; park just past the bus turning circle and the signed entry to *Knocklofty Reserve*

Bus: Metro route 5F (4x/day) to Upper Forest Rd terminus or route 5 and ask driver to stop

Lindisfarne from Knocklofty

4 Knocklofty Reserve

Walk directions

1 Just up from the bus turning circle is an entrance to the reserve, which has been beautifully landscaped and is clearly signed. Follow a wide gravelled path uphill and ignore any downhill minor branches.

2 The building carrying some unusual graffiti is the old pump house for the water pipeline that comes from Lake Fenton, Mt Field NP, which forms part of Hobart's water supply. Keep left at the next Y-junction to continue uphill. There are some beautiful mature gum trees in this area and as the track levels off you will also see She Oaks. You will soon pass a car park at the top end of Forest Road on your left and a picnic table.

3 Shortly you will notice the sandstone layer, mentioned in the introduction, become visible on your left, just before a large picnic area and fenced lookout. From here you can enjoy expansive views across the city towards the CBD on your left and to the Sandy Bay marina and Wrest Point Casino on your right with Mt Nelson forming a backdrop on the far right. Keep left at the next Y-junction and follow the marker posts that direct you along the summit loop. Keep walking along a fence with wooden rails to another junction.

4 Keep left and soon the track begins to swing northwards, passes under some power lines and becomes rocky as it rises quite steeply. In this shady section of your walk you will notice a difference in the vegetation. Large Blue Gums are overhead with Saggs and, a little further along, the beautiful white Flag Iris beneath. The rock type has changed from sandstone to dolerite. After a while Mt Wellington will come into view on your left and as you reach the summit, the track curves to the right through open dry bushland. Keep right at the junction with the Mt Stuart track and left where a closed track comes in from the right.

5 At the flattish summit plateau there is, sadly no marker to reward your achievement. The bush is lovely up here though and you

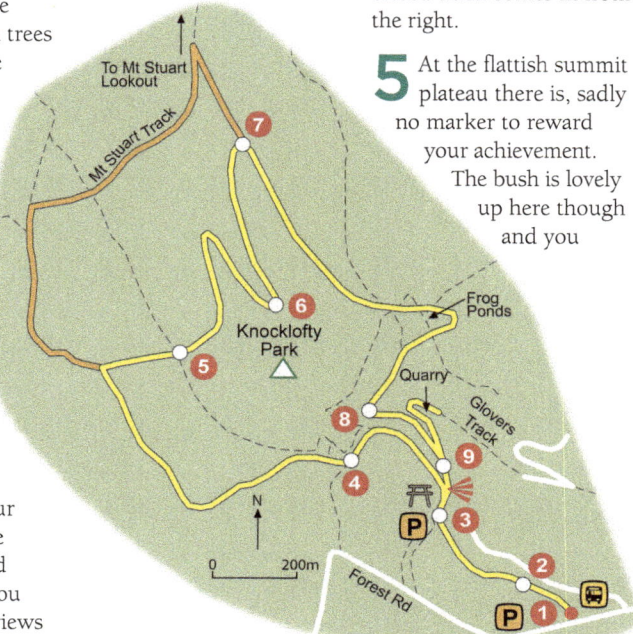

Walk Variations

You can include the Mt Stuart track (see map) for a longer circuit or begin the walk at the car park at the top end of Forest Road.

4 Knocklofty Reserve

can see northwards as far as Hobart's northern suburbs. Keep following the path and shortly the summit loop track turns right, back under power lines along a new, raised, gravelled section. You will walk through a small stand of She Oaks with its soft carpet of needles. In spring and summer everlastings can be seen in the rocky areas as the track begins to descend. Views of the Derwent Estuary and the Hobart CBD appear on your left. Continue until you reach a hairpin bend in the track.

6 In the bend, a short narrow pad leads to a delightful wooden 'chaise longue' which invites you to rest and enjoy the view. From here the track continues in a northerly direction to a T-junction.

7 Turn right and a few metres downhill, the track joins another track with a yellow marker. The track becomes steeper and the understorey plants become taller. Follow the track to another T-junction with an old vehicular track and continue straight ahead, across a grassy area with Stipa, Tussocks and Kangaroo Grass, towards a stand of trees to view the Frog Ponds. Curve right around a large Banksia (Bottlebrush) and walk past a large concrete reservoir on your left. You will see a small fenced area ahead. Walk along the wire fence

Hobart environment – the Eastern Barred Bandicoot

The Eastern Barred Bandicoot is a nocturnal marsupial that is now endangered. Its numbers have declined due to clearing of its natural habitat and hunting by domestic dogs and cats. It has soft, dense grey brown fur that is lighter underneath and has three lighter bands across the rump and a white tail. It is about forty centimetres long, with big ears and a very pointy nose which it uses to assist in digging for soil invertebrates such as cockchafer larvae, corbie grubs and earthworms. It supplements its diet with berries and bulbs in season. Females produce litters of up to four young which they keep in a rear-opening pouch. Young bandicoots become independent in three to five months after birth and can be seen following their mothers around for a while.

4 Knocklofty Reserve

8 A large interpretive sign along the track at the head of a gully, named Salvator Rosa Glen, depicts a painting by John Glover. It is thought that he sat here to paint it and it is interesting to compare the painting with the real landscape in front of you. The sandstone cliffs in the painting have been quarried since. Shortly after a sharp bend in the track, continue along the top of the gully. There's a track leading off to the left which goes down past one of the quarries in this gully and it is worth your while to wander down for a look. The sidetrack is named Glover's Track and eventually emerges at Poets Road.

to the interpretive sign about the six frog species that have been recorded here. Substantial plantings have been undertaken in this area to restore the bush and there are now many birds to be heard and seen. Continue on a gravelled path past another fenced area on your left and rejoin the vehicular track by turning left.

9 Back on the summit loop track you will soon return to the picnic area and fenced lookout you passed in point 3 and be able to retrace your steps from here.

Out and about - Knocklofty Hill

Knocklofty is part of the Mt Wellington foothills and forms the middle background for the western side of Hobart city centre. It was saved from the urban sprawl because it was considered too steep to build on in the early days of settlement. However, the sandstone for many of Hobart's early buildings, such as churches, banks and cottages was quarried from the eastern slopes of this area. At the same time the bush was used as a stock run and for firewood collection. The Hobart City Council purchased about 140 hectares on the skyline in 1942 to preserve this bush background for future generations. Alas, it became degraded until it was rescued by a local Bushcare group and with assistance from the Council it has become a beautiful vantage point from which to enjoy views across the CBD and to Sandy Bay.

5 Cascade Brewery, Gardens and Hobart Rivulet

In spring on this walk you will see beautiful displays of daffodils, rhododendrons and azaleas in the gardens, whereas in autumn coloured foliage of exotic deciduous trees such as birches, maples and poplars create splashes of colour. During the early 1800s, when Hobart was first settled, the rivulet was a vital source of drinking and washing water (it was also used to drive millwheels and served as a sewer!) The track follows the rivulet into the city. Return via a section of Macquarie Street, perhaps with a small detour for coffee. If you have extra time (about two hours) you can incorporate a visit to the brewery at the beginning or end of this walk.

At a glance

Grade: Easy
Time: 1 hr 40 mins return excluding climb to lookout
Distance: 4.4 km return
Ascent/descent: 40 m / 40 m
Conditions: Wide gravelled tracks, one steep ascent and descent, shady for much of the way
More info: www.hobartcity.com.au, Hobart City Council, Parks and Customer Service Division, T 6238 2886; the last section of the rivulet, which runs under the CBD, can be accessed by booking a tour with the Hobart City Council, T 6238 2711

Getting there
Car: Drive up Davey St, keeping right then turning right where it divides, then left into Cascade Rd; follow it until the distinctive historic façade of the Cascade Brewery building appears; Just before the brewery, turn right into a small car park
Bus: Metro route 49 stop 17

5 Cascade Brewery, Gardens and Hobart Rivulet

Walk directions

1 Take the main path through the gardens. The rivulet will be to your left, with a hill rising steeply behind it. Soon you will reach a fenced area that encloses a large concrete trash trap which catches logs and rocks that come down during flood times. The track curls around the right side of this pit and then crosses the creek towards a playground, picnic areas and public conveniences at the bottom of the gardens.

2 Exit through the car park and driveway, cross McRobies Road and walk straight ahead past the Female Factory sign onto the footpath of Degraves Street, lined with a row of Silver Birches. The high stone wall of the *Female Factory* site soon appears on the left.

3 Continue along the high stone wall of the Female Factory, passing a bridge across the rivulet on your right, until you see a fenced gravel track which leads along the rivulet with a scrap metal yard on your left. Some impressive sandstone cliffs will soon become visible through the trees on your left. You will reach a small river flat and pass a bridge to MacFarlane Street on your right. Young Blackwood trees line the edge of the path and during quiet times you can spot Native Hens here. At the far end of the cliffs the track rises steeply away from the rivulet to continue through bushland along the lower slopes of Knocklofty.

4 From the highest point on this track you can enjoy expansive views to South Hobart before you dip back down to the rivulet. Turn left to continue. A short time later pass a bridge to Anglesea Street and walk along a wooden paling fence and past a bridge to Weld Street. Shortly you also pass Wynyard Street and a small lawn and picnic area along a landscaped bank on your right to a BBQ area. Rusty

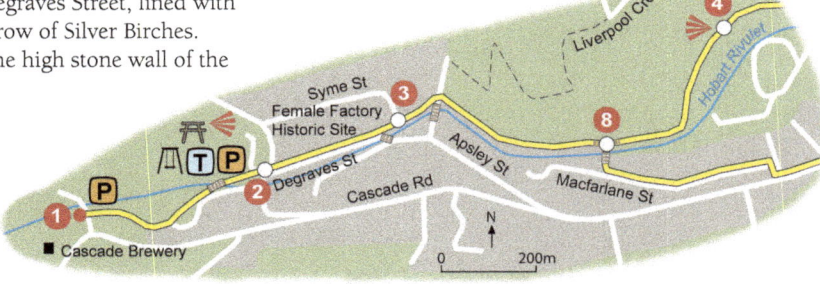

Hobart history – the Female Factory

This institution, also known as the Cascade Factory and House of Correction for Females was established in 1828 and operated for 28 years. Female convicts were sent here for punishment or while ill, awaiting childbirth or placement as servants. They were expected to work here, hence the name factory. A nursery was attached for the infants of convict mothers. In those days the area was swampy and the prison was overcrowded. Sanitation was poor and food and clothing inadequate. Disease and mortality rates were high particularly for infants. The complex was demolished in 1924 with only some remnants of the original walled yards and the Matron's cottage left standing. The site is open every day December to April 0900-1700 and May to November 0900-1600, guided tours can be booked, T 6223 1559.

5 Cascade Brewery, Gardens and Hobart Rivulet

Hobart geology – dolerite columns

During Jurassic times, when Gondwana split up, Tasmania went through very traumatic times, as it was almost torn in half. As a result, large amounts of magma rose through cracks in the earth's crust and spread mostly between layers of Triassic sandstones and Permian mudstones to form sills up to 450 metres thick. As the magma cooled it formed Tasmania's signature rock, the Jurassic Dolerite, only found in a few places on earth. Weathering has exposed the dolerite in its distinctive columns, a classic example being the 'Organ Pipes' on Mt Wellington, which form Hobart's backdrop.

steel structures across the rivulet were installed to catch logs after the devastating floods of 1960 when they had caused much destruction. On the opposite bank is the site of Vaucluse Gardens, which was once the mansion of businessman Thomas Hewitt. Later, from the early 1900s, it was used as a hospital before becoming part of the large Vaucluse Gardens Retirement Village that you see there now.

5 Cross Gore Street to the footpath along McKellar Street above the rivulet and a house. At the end of McKellar Street the track leads back down to the creek and shortly a tall brick chimney and the eastern entry to the park at the upper end of Collins Street become visible up ahead. Turn around and retrace your steps past Vaucluse Gardens. This time you will see Mt Wellington for much of the way.

6 Cross the rivulet at Wynyard Street and continue on the southern bank passing the playground and playing field of South Hobart School.

7 Turn left into Anglesea Street, then right into Macquarie Street. Pass Glen Street and turn right into Excell Lane then left into McFarlane Street. About halfway along it you can re-enter the rivulet linear park via the bridge you passed on your way downstream.

8 Retrace your steps to the lower end of Cascade gardens. A set of steps leads up the bank on your right just before the public conveniences for a short climb to a lookout, which is well worth the effort if you enjoy keeping fit. Perhaps it is now time for a cold beer!

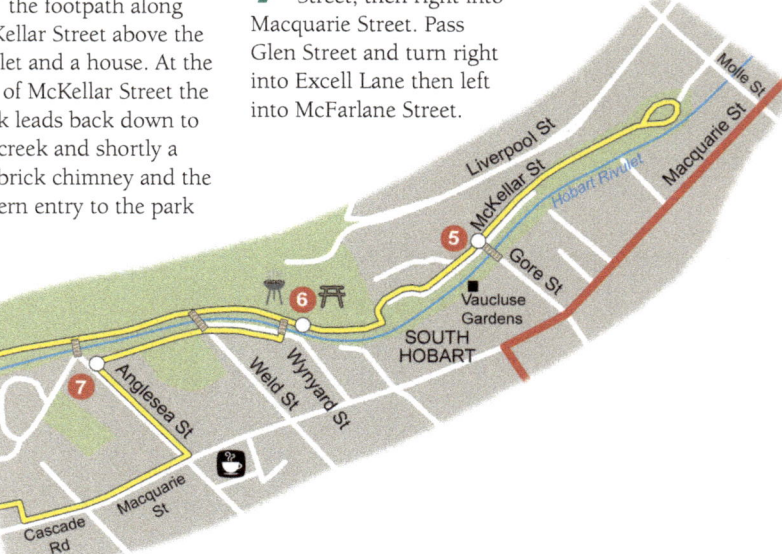

5 Cascade Brewery, Gardens and Hobart Rivulet

Out and about - Cascade Brewery

Australia's oldest continuously operating brewery was founded in 1824 by Peter Degraves and is surrounded by 250 hectares of bushland in the foothills of Mt Wellington. Originally the brewery was sited so that the pristine water flowing from the springs on Mt Wellington down the Hobart Rivulet could be used to make beers and ales, one of Hobart's earliest industries. The façade has retained its mid-Victorian tiered 'wedding cake' style, but the factory behind it has undergone continuous development. Tours are conducted several times per day. Contact the Woodstock Reception Centre across the road. For safety no children under 5, no walking aids, no shorts or skirts and strong shoes. T 6224 1117. Cost: adults $20, concessions $15, children, $10, families $45.

6 Mt Nelson Signal Station and Truganini Reserve

The start of this walk is not far from the Wrest Point Casino, a prominent landmark that can be seen from most vantage points in Hobart. The track follows Lambert Creek upstream along its west-facing bank through dry sclerophyll native bushland to the top of Mt Nelson, with its historic semaphore station, then past an Aboriginal Memorial and down along the shady, moist, south-facing bank of Cartwright Creek to meet Sandy Bay Road at the Grange picnic area, about ten kilometres south of the starting point. The easiest way to finish this interesting walk is to catch a bus back to the start at Lambert Avenue.

View from Signal Station across Derwent Estuary

At a glance

Grade: Medium/hard

Time: Lambert Ave to Signal Station 2 hrs; Truganini Reserve to Channel Hwy 45 mins

Distance: 2.9 km to Signal Station then 2 km through Truganini Reserve

Ascent/descent: 340 m / 340 m

Conditions: Well-defined tracks, steep in sections, mostly shady

More info: Hobart City Council, Parks & Customer Services Division, T 6238 2886, www.hobartcity.com.au

Getting there

Car: Take Sandy Bay Rd out of the city; just after Casino take the first turn right into Lambert Ave; park at top end

Bus: Routes 56, 61, 62, 63 from Franklin Sq to stop 15, or route 154 from Salamanca Pl, then walk to end of Lambert Ave

Return: car shuffle or bus Route 65 from Taroona - check with www.metrotas.com.au or hotline T 132201

6 Mt Nelson Signal Station and Truganini Reserve

Walk directions

1 Enter the reserve at the *Lambert Park* sign and walk straight ahead beneath some impressive Blue Gums. The track follows the upper bank of Lambert Creek. Keep right at a fork in the track and ignore a number of narrow side tracks that criss-cross the main path.

2 When you reach Churchill Avenue, which is a main thoroughfare and runs almost parallel to Sandy Bay Road below, turn right, cross the bridge and busy road to a large sign at the entry to Bicentennial Park. This connects Lambert Park with the Truganini Reserve. As you walk along the creek the banks gradually become steeper.

3 After a while you will cross the creek via a footbridge; the track becomes progressively steeper and rockier as it winds uphill skirting large dolerite boulders. Upper Sandy Bay's suburban back fences are visible on your left every now and then. Note how the vegetation changes from wet forest to dry sclerophyll forest, with White Gum, Prickly Box and the native Hop Bush with its shiny dark green leaves appearing in larger numbers.

4 Ignore a foot track crossing and keep right at the next Y-junction. An old vehicular track also crosses your path. Walk towards a large interpretation panel, which explains the reasons for control burns. Continue to climb towards a short wooden-railed walkway over a large storm water pipe. At this stage the views back to the city and Sandy Bay are a fine reward for your efforts. Across the gully you can catch sight of the suburb of Mt Nelson.

5 At the next Y-junction go left and follow signage to *Mt Nelson Signal Station*. As you climb higher more dry forest understorey plants appear, such as She Oaks, Wattle, Native Cherries and the low Correa bushes with their small bell shaped flowers. Pass the junctions with the ends of Euralla and Waymouth Avenues, keeping right. A couple of well-placed log seats invite you to rest and enjoy the views and the bush along

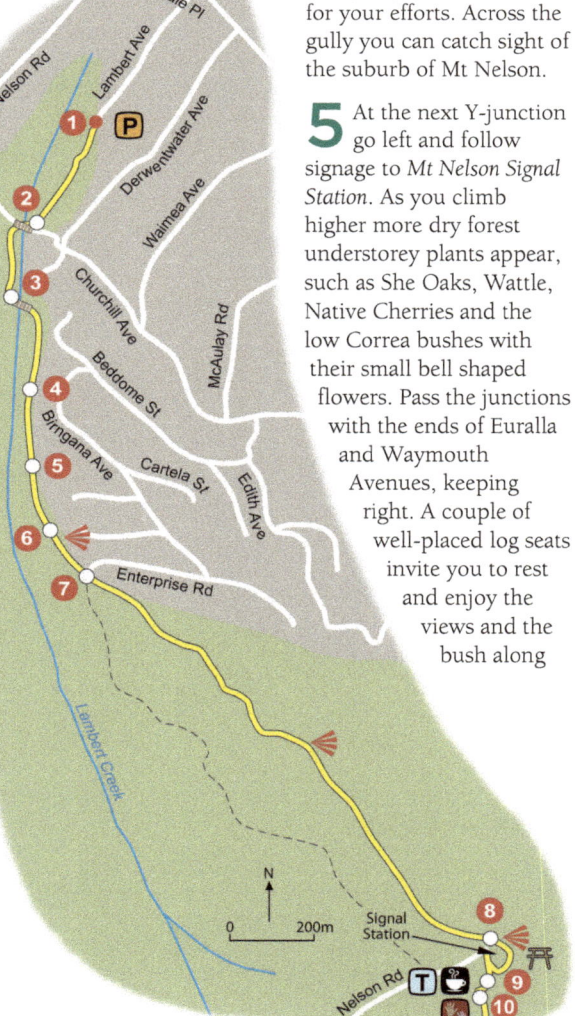

37

6 Mt Nelson Signal Station and Truganini Reserve

the way. Many endemic *Pimelia nivea* bushes can be found here, they have small, roundish, shiny dark green leaves with a velvety white underside.

6 After a while you come to a hairpin bend leading up to Acushla Court. Turn right and follow the well-defined track. A rather regal looking log seat on a low pedestal affords great views towards the summit of Mt Wellington. From here another hairpin bend in the track brings you up to the end of Enterprise Road.

7 Cross the road and continue on the track from which you can now glimpse the River Derwent through the trees. The track levels out considerably from here as you have already climbed about two thirds of the way. You will cross a couple of duckboarded wet spots in the open bushland. Stay on the wider gravelled track until several houses become visible through the trees on your right. Only a little further along you will arrive at a small viewing platform from where a wide bitumen path winds up to the signal station, the Signalman's Cottage and the turning circle at the end of Nelson Road and it will become obvious to you why it was built here!

8 Take some time to explore the area, enjoy the panoramic views and have a well earned rest. The nearby Station Café opens Tues–Fri 1000-1600, Sat-Sun 1000-1700, for reservations T 6223 3407.

9 Locate the Truganini Reserve track behind the Signalman's Cottage, which is well signposted and leads down to the left past a timber post and rail fence and under a stand of magnificent old Blue Gums. Shortly a sign will point to the Aboriginal Memorial which is at a small dolerite outcrop. Two bench seats allow time for reflection.

Walk variations

Many of these are possible depending on time available and your degree of fitness. For example you can visit Mt Nelson Signal Station and Truganini Reserve separately as one way walks either up or downhill using bus services or car shuffles to return to your starting point. You can also enter Bicentennial Park from Eurella Avenue, Waymouth Avenue or Acushla Court in upper Sandy Bay or from Bends 2 and 4 on Nelson Road.

6 Mt Nelson Signal Station and Truganini Reserve

10 Return to the track which becomes steep and rocky as it descends down the south facing slope of Mt Nelson into the shady, moist gully that was formed by Cartwright Creek. These conditions support a very different set of plants to the dry hillside you climbed earlier. As you near the valley floor, the bush assumes a rainforest feel with ferns and mosses, tea-tree, Native Currant and Dogwood in the understorey and the voices of Crescent Honeyeaters, Olive Whistlers and Currawongs in the Blue Gums above. Beware of the round log steps as the moist environment makes them very slippery.

Hobart history - Mt Nelson Signal Station

The semaphore signal station at Mt Nelson was named for the ship *Lady Nelson* which brought the first settlers into Hobart. It was established in 1811 to relay messages from two separate circuits to Battery Point (see point 6 of Walk 1). The first circuit notified the movement of ships in and out of the port of Hobart to marine authorities; the second linked the penal colony of Port Arthur with Hobart. When Port Arthur was closed in 1877, the relevant circuit of signals was removed. The system of signal stations became obsolete with the arrival of the modern telephone in 1880.

6 Mt Nelson Signal Station and Truganini Reserve

11 When you reach Cartwright Creek cross then re cross it and continue the steep descent until the gully widens and the track becomes less rocky. The track is well defined all along the way and finally emerges at a *Truganini Reserve* sign and a Y-junction. Keep left and shortly you will reach another *Truganini Walking Track* sign and a fire trail. Follow this out to the *The Grange* picnic area on the Channel Highway. Turn left to locate bus stop no 32 for your return journey to Lambert Avenue. Take great care as there is no footpath. Take the bus back to stop 15 and return to the start.

6 Mt Nelson Signal Station and Truganini Reserve

Hobart people - Truganini

When Tuganini died in 1876 it meant that the last Tasmanian Aboriginal full-blood had died, as she had no living relatives and no children of her own. However it did not mean the death of Aboriginality in Tasmania, as descendants of mixed blood from other Tasmanian tribes still live in Tasmania today. There is no certainty about her year of birth but it is thought to have been either 1803 or 1812. She was the daughter of Mangerner, chief of the Recherche Bay people. Her mother is said to have been stabbed to death by sealers. There are a number of conflicting stories about her life. When she died, her skeleton was acquired by the Royal Society of Tasmania - against her explicit wishes. A hundred years later, after a long legal battle, her bones were returned to the Aboriginal community for cremation and her ashes were scattered in the D'Entrecasteaux Channel.

7 Alexandra Battery and Lower Sandy Bay

This is a very pleasant family walk where children can explore the tunnels and nooks and crannies of the historic Alexandra Battery, a rocky waterfront with the famous 'Blinking Billy' lighthouse and a beautiful beach. At Sandown Park there is plenty of room to play and a large, attractive, fenced playground with lots of rocking, climbing and swinging gear. The area has plenty of shaded seating where you can enjoy a relaxed picnic lunch, breathe the clean sea air, watch the myriad of boats and take in the scenery. There are also a number of eateries nearby to suit all tastes.

At a glance

Grade: Easy
Time: 1 hr return, but allow much more with children
Distance: 3 km circuit
Conditions: Exposed at Alexandra Battery, some shade along promenade
More info: Hobart City Council, Parks and Customer Service Division, T 6238 2886, www.hobartcity.com.au

Getting there

Car: From Sandy Bay Rd turn right into Nelson Rd just before the Casino and then left into Churchill Ave; park when you see Alexandra Battery Park on your left (~7.5 km)
Bus: Metro routes 51, 52, 53, 54 to Alexandra Battery

Alexandra Battery

7 Alexandra Battery and Lower Sandy Bay

Walk directions

1 To get a good overview of the walk, climb the small lookout adjacent to the car park. From here you can see Sandy Bay Point and Long Beach to your left and, further to the right, Blinking Billy Point. Just below are the lawns of the Alexandra Battery Park. Walk down the lawns towards the first fenced area slightly to your left. Go down some stone steps to find a tunnel, about 30 metres long, that leads down into the main area where there are three gun emplacements that once had canons bolted to them. Kids love exploring this area. Exit through heavy gates towards the lower right side of the site.

2 Turn left and walk along the bottom fence until you see a foot track leading down to Sandy Bay Road. Carefully cross the busy road and continue on the other side. Shortly after, turn right into a lane (between houses) that obviously leads down to the coast.

7 Alexandra Battery and Lower Sandy Bay

3 At the end of this lane is Blinking Billy Reserve, which was originally called One Tree Point. Turn right and you will see the little lighthouse perched on the bank just past a concrete shed. Take the narrow track that passes below it to get a better look, then turn back to continue your walk along the coast towards Long Beach.

4 Head past the Longbeach Bathing Pavilion and a BBQ area to reach the end of Beach Road and Sandown Park. This has hockey and soccer playing fields, beautiful children's playground and revamped promenade. This whole area has recently been re-developed to strengthen the foreshore and upgrade facilities. It is now a pleasant place to stop and rest. Nearby Beach Road has a coffee shop, Bakery and takeaways.

5 Continue your walk along the shore around Sandy Bay Point past the Regatta Pavilion and take a narrow path through a few shrubs to emerge at Nutgrove Beach. Walk along the beach past the Sailing Club building.

6 A little further on turn left through a wind barrier into a narrow lane between a house to the right and a wire fence to the left. When you reach the corner of Beechworth Road and Sandown Avenue, walk along Sandown Avenue until you come to a small car park.

Hobart history - Blinking Billy

The One Tree Point Light as it was known during its years of operation from 1900 to 1955, was built and maintained as an aid to navigation. The first Tasmanian ship to shore transmission was made in July 1901 between HMS St George and Long Beach Light Station. Sir Geoffry Walch was instrumental in the preservation of this lighthouse as a landmark.

7 Alexandra Battery and Lower Sandy Bay

7 Turn left and head back towards the waterfront, passing under some giant Blue Gum trees that house many different bird species such as Eastern Rosellas, Swift Parrots and Magpies.

8 Back on the promenade turn right, then right again into Beach Road. Cross Sandy Bay Road at the traffic lights, turn left and then right to walk up Wayne Avenue. After about 100 metres turn left into a lane which has a hedge along it. A series of steps lead back up to the Alexandra Battery lawns and the car park at the top.

Sandown Park

Hobart history - Alexandra Battery

Named in honour of Princess Alexandra of Denmark, the battery was completed in 1885, in response to an unexplained visit by three Russian naval ships in the River Derwent in 1873. It was, together with two other batteries, one near the Cenotaph and the other at Kangaroo Bluff on the Eastern Shore, designed to defend Hobart from invasion. Thankfully there was never a shot fired in anger from any of the batteries and by 1903 they became (even more) obsolete when the Commonwealth took over defence matters. It has fine views over the Derwent River.

8 Waterworks and Pipeline Track

This walk leads you to one of Hobart's favourite picnic spots and playgrounds, with large lawn areas shaded by mature trees overlooking the two reservoirs and Mt Wellington as a backdrop. Ducks and Native Hens as well as wallabies can be spotted, particularly mornings or late afternoons. You will also find an excellent display about Hobart's water supply system during early settlement and information on the remnants of it to be found along the track. A bus ride up the mountain to Ferntree to avoid a steep climb is included to add interest to the walk. A number of short walks can also be undertaken or incorporated into this walk from here. Consult the map outside the receiving house.

It is essential to check Metro bus services along Huon Road from stop 21 to Ferntree such as route 48 or combinations of other routes (T 132201) before setting out on the walk so that you can arrange to get to the bus stop at the right time. You may want to start or finish your walk with a barbecue meal or picnic.

Old aqueduct

At a glance

Grade: medium
Time: From site 9 to bus stop 21 – 20 to 25 mins; from Ferntree back to start point 50 to 60 mins
Distance: 1.2 km from site 9 to bus stop 21; 3.4 km from Ferntree to Waterworks
Ascent/descent: 80 m / 270 m
Conditions: Well-defined tracks throughout; note that the park opens at 0830 and closes at 1615 in winter, 0800-2100 during daylight saving time in summer
More info: Hobart City Council - Parks & Customer Service Division, T 6238 2886, www.hobartcity.com.au

Getting there

Car: Drive up Davey St to where it divides; DO NOT turn left but keep straight ahead and take the first road to the left (Romily St) shortly after passing a roundabout; follow signage to *Waterworks Reserve* and drive along both reservoirs to picnic site No 9

Bus: Route 470 is infrequent, but you can simply start the walk from Ferntree (see point 4 and then from Waterworks Reserve walk back to Huon Road to catch a bus (waypoints 1-3)

8 Waterworks and Pipeline Track

Walk directions

1 An historic stone building, the original receiving house, is clearly visible near the starting point at picnic site number 9. It is worthwhile taking some time to step inside and view the informative display which will give you a good overview about the history of the pipeline and what you are about to find on this walk. When you are done, walk on to site 10 and the top end of the upper reservoir where you will see a planting of manferns and the start of the walking track.

2 Walk to the left of the manferns to a fork in the track and turn right. The track snakes through the bushland along the upper reserve. Follow it until you reach a junction with a wider, bitumen vehicular track.

3 Turn left and follow it uphill until you reach the Huon Road near a water pump station. Turn left just before the station and walk along the track inside the roadside fence until a gap in the fence leads to bus stop No 21.

4 Take the bus to Ferntree. Ask the driver to stop at the beginning of *Wellington Walking Tracks*. The stone bus shelter at this stop is a gem which is to be admired in its own right. Its furnishings reflect the kindly nature of the locals. This small community is 430 metres above sea level and was devastated by the 1967 bushfires that raged in much of southern Tasmania. Miraculously, the small wooden church you can see across the road escaped the flames. Ferntree has a tavern and a general store where takeaways and drinks are also available.

5 To continue your walk, locate the start of the pipeline track by following the wooden picket fence down from the bus stop. In the centre of the track you can still see the old stone slabs which cover the aqueduct. The steps down this track

Pipeline track

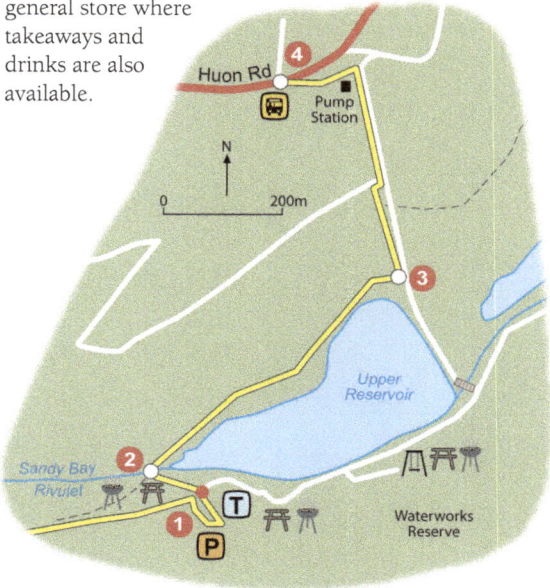

8 Waterworks and Pipeline Track

can be very slippery, but a handrail is provided. Only a few minutes away is the Longhill aqueduct where the pipeline crosses Dunns Creek (which was formerly named Longhill Creek). Continue on the well-marked track to follow the pipeline on its way down. Soon you will come to another beautifully built aqueduct.

6 From here the track levels out. Follow it until you emerge at Halls Saddle, which is where Chimney Pot Road from Ridgeway joins the Huon Highway. There is a picnic shelter and small car park to your right, and across the road the continuation of the Pipeline Track.

7 Follow it past a well-built, stylish historic stone valve house. In spring and summer many beautiful flowering native shrubs such as Pimelia, Epacris and Correa can be admired along the way. You will also be able to see across to Mt Wellington on your left.

Pipeline

Hobart environment - Tasmanian Native Hens

Endemic to Tasmania, these are the size of a swamphen, have yellow beaks, red eyes and are olive-brown in colour with dark undersides and white patches on their flanks. They are commonly found in marshes and river flats, near creeks and rivers. They can't fly but swim well and run very fast. Some have been clocked at 50 km per hour! Native Hens are very social and several will often make a shrill 'naarkee-naarkee-narkee' alarm call in unison.

8 Waterworks and Pipeline Track

8 The track curves gently around the western side of Chimney Pot Hill until it reaches Mc Dermotts Saddle which was once a farm. Follow signage to Gentle Annie Falls. Just before the falls the track becomes rocky before you arrive at a fenced lookout above the falls - which are mostly dry. Hand-hewn sandstone steps lead down the side of the falls, which consist of two separate drops.

9 At the base of the second drop you can admire this engineering feat of the 1800s before turning sharp left at the end of the steel handrail for a gentle stroll under a small stand of Silver Peppermint Gums, veering right down into a beautiful, shady little gully from where you will be able to see some more sand stone cliffs. Keep left at a Y-junction before emerging at the manfern planting, No 9 picnic area and your start point.

Hobart history - Hobart Waterworks

Water shortages and illnesses arising from poor water quality necessitated the building of this water scheme by the early 1860s. The basic scheme drew water from the Ferntree Bower area and included the carved sandstone section of Gentle Annie Falls and the receiving house at the Waterworks Reserve. Over the next forty years, as the need arose, the scheme was extended to include the Plains Rivulet and the North West Bay River. Later on water was piped from Lake Fenton at Mt Field, north-west of Hobart and an old pumphouse on this line can be seen at the beginning of Walk 4, Knocklofty Reserve. Today only twenty per cent of water comes from Mt Wellington, twenty per cent from Mt Field and the remaining sixty per cent from the upper reaches of the Derwent River.

The Eastern Shore and South Arm Peninsula

Some of the best views of Hobart's city centre and the Wellington Range can be enjoyed from the Eastern Shore suburbs of Geilston Bay, Lindisfarne, Rose Bay, Montagu Bay, Rosny and Bellerive. These suburbs are clustered around four prominent hills that stand between the River Derwent and the Meehan Range. They are Natone Hill, Gordons Hill, Rosny Hill and Mornington Hill. You will climb and become acquainted with three of these hills during the walks in this chapter, as their summits have all been made into reserves. Very dry conditions and different rock types determine the vegetation communities and hence the birds and animals you will find on these hills.

The last three walks in this chapter lead you down the 'arm' extension of Hobart's Eastern Shore, which juts into the Derwent Estuary.

Arm End

9 Shag Bay

This is a pleasant coastal walk that initially leads along the edge of Geilston Bay and then the Bedlam Walls, which are the top edge of a deep crack in the earth's crust that extends right along the River Derwent. Next you will skirt around the edge of Shag Bay, a small, narrow bay with panoramic views of the River Derwent, extending to the Tasman Bridge and across to New Town Bay and the suburb of Lutana. Rock quarried from Shag Bay was used to build Macquarie Wharf in Hobart. The track rises to the top of Fishers Hill from where you will see, across the river, one of the largest factories in Tasmania, locally known as the Zinc Works. Along the way you will also find a very local endemic Eucalypt.

At a glance

Grade: Easy/medium
Time: 1 hr 25 m
Distance: 4.8 km return
Ascent/descent: 90 m /90 m
Conditions: Clear tracks, open and exposed in some sections; short climbs
More info: Parks and Wildlife Service, South East Division, T 6214 8100

Getting there
Car: From the East Derwent Hwy, turn into Geilston Bay Rd and park in a small car park at its end, just before a barred gravel road
Bus: Routes 680, 685, 690, 692, 694 to Geilston Bay Rd and walk up to start point (< 1 km)

Geilston Bay

9 Shag Bay

Walk directions

1 Just before a yellow barrier turn left down a foot track signed *Heritage Trail* which leads downhill to follow the edge of Geilston Bay, where a number of yachts are usually moored. As you walk along the track the forest becomes more open with Blue Gums and a grassy understorey with Saggs. There are soon views down the Derwent towards the Tasman Bridge on your left.

2 At a y-junction keep left and walk along the narrower track, that leads along the coast, until you get to the top of some fenced timber steps which lead steeply down the cliffs. Part of this track is currently closed, but you can still see some of the caves that once sheltered the Mou-maire-mener band of the local indigenous Oyster Bay Tribe. From the lookout walk uphill until you come to a junction of 4 tracks.

3 Take the second one from the left, which leads towards Shag Bay. You will pass under a power line before a short, steep descent that leads onto the flat rocky shelves that line this side of Shag Bay.

Shag Bay, Cave Lookout

9 Shag Bay

You can walk along these shelves until you see a rusty old steel cylinder, part of the remnants of a chemical fertiliser factory which exploded in 1915. The factory was never rebuilt because shortly afterwards the Electrolytic Zinc Company, which manufactured superphosphate fertiliser as a by-product of its zinc-making processes, was established across the River Derwent in Lutana.

4 Just before the cylinder some wooden steps lead up the bank and then continue along it to go to the head of the bay.

5 From here the track rises sharply along the northern side of Shag Bay to go to the top of Fishers Hill. You will pass a rocky outcrop in the dry sclerophyll bushland which is also home to a very local Gum tree species, *Eucalyptus risdonii*.

6 When you reach the power transmission lines which run overhead, you will be able to look across to the Zinc Works, a major employer for Hobartians. A good specimen of Risdon Peppermint can be found along the track just 20 metes south of the transmission line. Retrace your steps as far as the four way junction and from there continue on the wider main path straight ahead, which will lead you back to the start of the walk.

Hobart history - The Zinc Works

The Electrolytic Zinc Works were established in 1916 - zinc supplies from Germany were disrupted by WWI and, as zinc was a vital ingredient in munitions production, it became necessary for Australia to produce its own. Luckily the electrolytic method had just been developed to produce zinc cheaply and the huge amounts of electricity necessary for this process were available through Tasmania's new hydro-electric scheme. Zinc ore came from Broken Hill and Rosebery in Tasmania and production started in 1918. By the 1920s the plant ran 24 hours a day and employed 1300 workers; employment peaked in 1967 with 2800 workers when Risdon was the world's second largest zinc refinery. In the 1970s the Derwent was found to be polluted and the Zinc Works was blamed amid much publicity. The Company managed to control pollution and production has continued, though with a much-reduced workforce. The Risdon Plant is now controlled by Zinifex.

9 Shag Bay

Hobart environment - Risdon Peppermint (*Eucalyptus risdonii*)

During this walk you can find this small gum tree species on the low hill between Geilston and Shag Bays and on Fishers Hill. Its description was first published in 1847. It only grows on mudstone soils on the northern side of the Derwent River and its habitat is small and localised, extending only as far as Cambridge. Where stands have been burnt it develops a shrubby habit, otherwise it is a small tree. Its juvenile leaves cling to the branches without a stem and are very glaucous (whitish-blue, waxy).

Shag Bay

10 Lindisfarne Bay and Gordons Hill

Enjoy the magnificent panoramic views from Hobart's Eastern Shore across the River Derwent towards the city nestled under Mt Wellington. Walking along the foreshore you will get an increasingly closer look at the Tasman Bridge, pass under it and - from a pedestrian overpass - get a bird's eye view along the bridge as well. A short, invigorating climb up Gordons Hill with its calming Casuarina woodland and grassy top and a descent via some suburban streets complete this circuit.

M W Simmons Park

At a glance

Grade: Easy/medium
Time: A little over 2 hrs
Distance: 6.8 km circuit
Ascent/descent: 130 m / 130 m
Conditions: Bike and walk tracks, pebbly coast, some streets and bush tracks
More info: Clarence City Council, T 6245 8600, www.ccc.tas.gov.au

Getting there

Car: From the East Derwent Hwy heading north, turn left into very short Bay St; cross the Lindisfarne Esp diagonally, towards the left side of the Lindisfarne Rowing Club, and into a car park

Bus: Routes 680, 685, 690, 692, 694 to Stop 10 - walk a short distance along the East Derwent Hwy then turn left into Bay Street and on to the car park

10 Lindisfarne Bay and Gordons Hill

Walk directions

1 From the car park take the bitumen shared bike/pedestrian track which leads through M. W. Simmons Park along the head of the bay. The views across the river are expansive from here. Exit the park at the far end, turn right and walk along the Esplanade, crossing Ballawinne Road.

2 At the second jetty, step down to the pebbly foreshore to continue your walk along it. (On the very rare occasions that water

Hobart history – the Tasman Bridge

When the decision was made in the 1960s to build a new piered bridge across the Derwent it was thought that this would be a straightforward job. However, it was soon found that while piers hit solid dolerite near the eastern shore, some piers near the centre just disappeared in mud, due to the huge rift below the river. Piers had to be extended and splayed beneath the water level to carry the bridge and several piers do not have a solid footing.

Looking at the bridge today you will note that a pier is missing near the eastern shore. This is due to the tragic event in 1975 when the bulk ore carrier *Lake Illawarra* accidentally missed the central navigation span and ran into two piers near the eastern shore. The piers collapsed along with about 125 metres of bridge decking. Four cars plunged into the Derwent River and five occupants lost their lives while several others managed to escape from two vehicles which teetered on the edge of the gap. Seven crewmen from the *Lake Illawarra* also lost their lives. The ship still lies under the gap, a new pier could not be built over the top of it and you can see the wider span when you look at the bridge.

10 Lindisfarne Bay and Gordons Hill

levels are too high to allow this, continue along the esplanade.) Cross a disused boat ramp and, at Shore Street Point, pass a small rocky outcrop which shows some weathered basalt underneath a thick layer of Pleistocene gravels. Next you will encounter some interesting 'paving' as you near the Tasman Bridge. When you reach a stone embankment on your left, step up and onto the *Clarence Foreshore Trail* which begins here at Rose Bay.

3 Follow the trail as it winds past parking areas, lawn and seating on the left. As you near the bridge the track runs along the back fences of suburban houses until it emerges at the end of Rose Bay Esplanade. Continue along here to a junction with a vehicle track. Cross this and take the track to the right which leads under the Tasman Bridge - a great spot to get close and familiar with this Hobart icon.

4 From here the foreshore track continues between a playing field on the left and a fenced yard of the SES. The track descends to Montagu Bay, with its views of Sullivans Cove and Hobart CBD, through a small stand of She-oaks. Cross over the grassed area to the Rosny Esplanade and turn left.

5 At the end of the esplanade turn right into Conara Road then right again into Riawena Road. Take the next left turn up Lonah Road and walk uphill towards the East Derwent Highway.

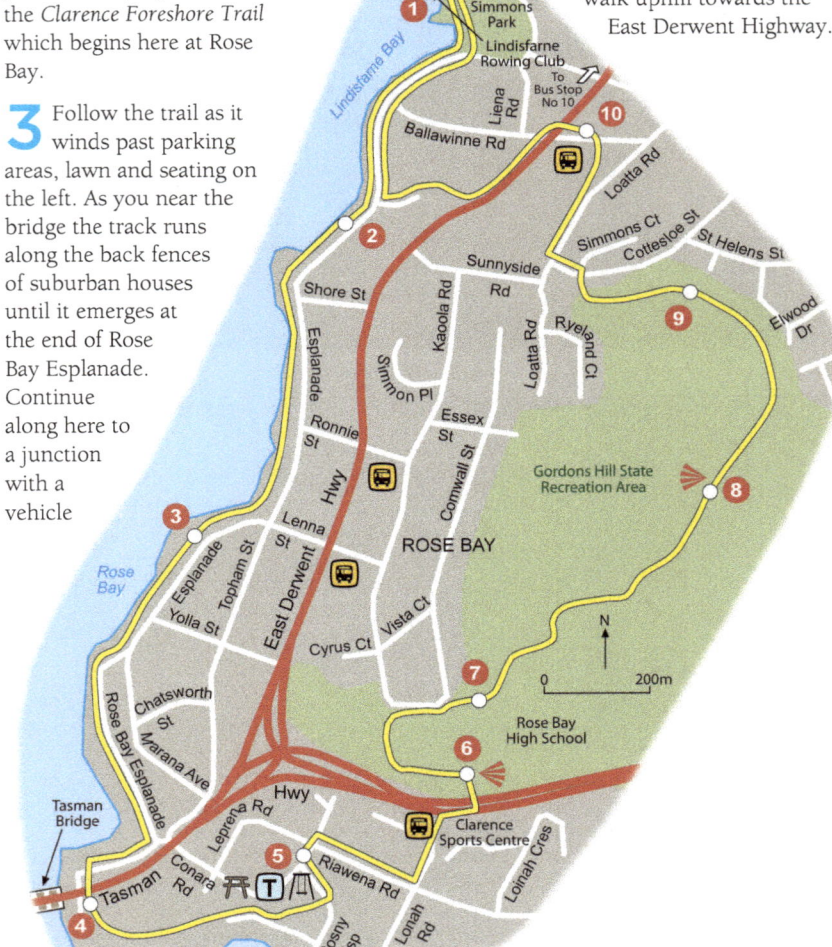

10 Lindisfarne Bay and Gordons Hill

Montagu Bay

Turn right when you see a pedestrian overpass and use it to cross the highway. It serves as a fantastic lookout along the highway towards the bridge, the Queen's Domain, Government Hourse and the city. You can see Montagu Bay below and to its left Rosny Hill.

6 Having crossed the highway turn left and walk along the front, side and back of Rose Bay High School, enjoying the spectacular views from this area. From the far back corner of the school head up a bitumen path, leaving the school's playing field to your right, leading uphill into the bush straight ahead. Walk through a couple of boulder barriers. Soon you will note a large blue sign - *Gordons Hill Nature Recreation Area* - and a panel about the Eastern Barred Bandicoot.

7 Enter the narrow foot track which now leads uphill. Ignore a track to

10 Lindisfarne Bay and Gordons Hill

the right, keeping straight ahead and uphill through the beautiful She-oak woodland which also contains Prickly Box. This has heart-shaped seedpods and sweetly scented white spring-time flowers that are good for honey production. Ignore another foot track that crosses and follow the trail which winds to the right and then left and in a while becomes steeper and rockier. The understorey grass now contains tussocks and other native grasses and there are a few Blue Gums overhead as you near the top of the hill. The rock underfoot is dolerite.

8 The summit is a small, clear, grassy area - a good place to rest a while. There are particularly good views up the Derwent northwards. You can see Selfs Point with its large white tanks and beyond the Zinc Works. It is clear where the bandicoots have been and if you are lucky you will spot one. At the Y-junction take the fairly faint right track which leads towards a large dead gumtree. Just before the gum turn right into a faint vehicular track which leads northeast and downhill. Shortly the track becomes more defined. When you see a paling fence up ahead you will come to a three-way junction.

9 Turn left into a narrow foot track which, at first, runs along

Cyclist on Gordons Hill

the contour of Gordons Hill then gently descends. Further down cross another vehicle track and continue downhill along wooden paling fences and through a narrow lane between houses onto Cottesloe Street. You will get a clear view of Lindisfarne Bay from here. Turn left and then right into Loatta Road. When you reach a large playing field, walk towards the traffic lights on the East Derwent Highway, diagonally opposite.

10 Cross here and turn left. After passing the Lindisfarne Motor Inn, locate a narrow lane on the right, two power poles along, which leads down to Selbourne Place. Go down the steps and straight ahead to the esplanade. Turn right and retrace your steps to the start point.

10 Lindisfarne Bay and Gordons Hill

11 Rosny Hill Lookout and Foreshore

A grandstand view of the city and Tasman Bridge are the best features of this pleasant and easy walk along the Rosny foreshore, mostly on bitumen a shared bicycle/walking track.

At a glance

Grade: Easy/medium
Time: 1¼ hrs
Distance: 4.2 km circuit
Ascent/descent: 60 m / 60 m
Conditions: One short steep climb; narrow, overgrown link track to the lookout may be a challenge to locate; mostly shaded
More info: Clarence City Council, T 6245 8600, www.ccc.tas.gov.au

Getting there

Car: Take the Tasman Hwy to the Eastern Shore, turn right into Riawena Rd then turn left into Bastick St; park in *Public Boat Launching Ramp Car Par*k

Bus: Routes 602, 670, 675 to Rosny Point

11 Rosny Hill Lookout and Foreshore

Walk directions

1 Walk diagonally across the Bowling Club car park, cross Bastick Street and locate a set of concrete steps between houses 45 and 47. Go up the steps to Leura Street.

2 Turn right and enter the short foot track into the signed *Rosny Hill Nature Recreation Area*, leading onto Haven Court. Before entering the Court, take a rough vehicle track which switches back on the left and goes uphill. Follow it until you reach a fire trail.

3 Turn left to follow the fire trail between suburban back yards and the Blue Gum and She-oak bushland that covers most of the top of Rosny Hill. There are commanding views over Kangaroo Bay and the South Arm Peninsula on the left and Mt Nelson across the River Derwent on the right. The trail leads into the edge of the tree area as it follows the contour of the hill.

4 When the track begins to dip down slightly, and just before it goes back out into the open grassed area, locate the narrow, slightly overgrown foot track on the right, opposite two small tree stumps. Turning sharp right, follow the trail uphill to reach the bitumen summit road after about 80 metres. There's a large interpretive panel here titled *Looking out on history*, which is about Hobart's first settlement of 262 souls in 1804. There is also some information about the early ferries that made it possible to farm the rich eastern plains of Clarence and Richmond.

5 Turn left and follow the summit loop road along the car parking spaces, from which you can enjoy one of Hobart's best views, especially of the city and the Tasman Bridge.

6 When you reach a small car park on your left, just down from the summit, turn left and downhill onto an old grassy

63

11 Rosny Hill Lookout and Foreshore

vehicle track. Follow this until you reach a Y-junction and turn left. The track leads down onto Kellatie Road.

7 Cross it then continue downhill via a narrow lane between two paling fences to the left of a power pole. The lane leads down to Hesket Court.

8 Turn right and walk down the court to its junction with Rosny Esplanade. Cross this diagonally towards the Tasman Bridge and enter the bitumen shared bicycle/walking foreshore track by turning left. More wonderful vistas open up as the track winds along the foreshore. The track eventually rounds Rosny Point and Kangaroo Bay will come into view.

9 The path makes a short detour around a sewage treatment plant, passes the end of Seabird Lane and finally winds through a small stand of She-oaks before emerging at the start point.

View from Rosny to Bellerive

11 Rosny Hill Lookout and Foreshore

View from Rosny foreshore to City

Hobart people - Walter Angus Bethune

Walter Bethune, the holder of the original land grant which included Rosny Hill, named Rosny after his ancestor, the Duc de Maximilien de Bethune Sully, of Rosny near Mantes in France. Bethune (1794-1885) was born in Scotland and visited Van Diemen's Land in 1820 returning the following year with his wife Barbara. He established himself as a merchant in Hobart Town, ran a counting house and also a whaling base at Slopen Island, amassing several city allotments and country holdings. Bethune became the director of the Bank of Van Diemen's Land and of the Commercial Bank of Tasmania and settled permanently on his 25,000 acre estate *Dunrobin* near Ouse. His sheep were well bred from pure English stock and highly sought after by new settlers. You will find quite a few names with French connections in Tasmania, as described further in the Bruny Island chapter.

12 Rosny to Bellerive Beach

Travel back in time with a visit to the little known, quaint Rosny Historic Centre, then walk to Bellerive village and enjoy the liveliness of the Bellerive Boardwalk and Quay with its myriad yachts. Continue, in Charles Darwin's footsteps, along the foreshore track from which you can see into the clear, shallow waters that lap the long rocky shelf along the shore and which are a favourite fishing ground for water birds. Detour to the old fort on Bellerive Bluff and wander along Bellerive Beach to Second Bluff. Return via a walking track behind the dunes and quiet suburban streets.

Bellerive Quay

At a glance

Grade: Medium

Time: 2½ hrs; allow much more for viewing historic centre, fort and foreshore

Distance: 8.3 km circuit

Ascent/descent: 20 m / 20 m

Conditions: Pavement and well constructed walking tracks

More info: Rosny Historic Centre opens Tues–Fri 1100–1600, Sat–Sun 1200–1600, T 6245 8740

Getting there

Car: From the East Derwent Hwy take the *Eastlands, Historic Centre, Golf Course* exit and park at the highway end of the supermarket car park, (4 hrs limit)

Bus: Routes 606, 613, 615, 620, 625, 630, 642, 650, 652, 660, 662, 665, 685, 694 to Rosny overpass, stop 13

12 Rosny to Bellerive Beach

Walk directions

1 Walk uphill past the bottle shop and cross the entry to the supermarket car park towards the Historic Centre and Golf Course car park. An interpretive sign and the entrance to the Rosny Historic Centre appear on your right.

2 The centre is administered by the local council and consists of an old stone farm barn built in 1815, a sandstone cottage and a weatherboard schoolhouse gallery with local art work as well as a small garden planted with Tasmanian native plants.

The inside of the cottage is fully furnished and equipped with household items as though it was still in use. It is a credit to managers and visitors that there are no bars and you can wander around freely to inspect the exhibits. From the Centre turn right

Bellerive Beach

Hobart history - Bellerive Wharf

After the Tasman Bridge disaster in 1975, Hobart's Eastern Shore residents were suddenly cut off from the city's vital services and, in many cases, their workplaces as well (the long detour via the Bridgewater bridge to the north was not a viable long term option). The obvious solution was to revitalise the ferry service. The Sullivans Cove Ferry Company started its service within hours of the disaster and by the next day three private ferries and one government ferry began their services. Queues of commuters were long and a private ship builder saw a business opportunity to build high-speed catamarans for the river crossing. Incat went on to become one of Tasmania's main employers, exporting their vessels all over the world. The bridge took nearly three years to rebuild. Other legacies of the disaster include more commercial and public facilities on the Eastern Shore and the Bowen Bridge upstream at Risdon.

12 Rosny to Bellerive Beach

pedestrian overpass and continue on the other side towards the bay.

3 On your right is the Charles Hand Memorial Park, which hosts the annual Christmas Carols by Candlelight ceremony on its expansive lawns, drawing crowds of thousands.

4 Keep left at a Y-junction and walk through a small rose garden. The large building on your right is Rosny College. The park merges into the Kangaroo Bay Sports Ground; cross diagonally towards the water. When you see a track, which is shared with bicycles, turn left and continue along the shore through Kangaroo Park. Soon you will reach the Bellerive Quay. Continue along it past the ferry wharf to the car park.

5 Join the start of the *Clarence Foreshore Trail*. A small boulder with a plaque and a map about the Charles Darwin Trail, of which this trail is a part, marks its entry. Charles Darwin is said to have walked along this shore and to the top of Mornington Hill to the northeast (see walk 13) when he visited Hobart in 1836.

6 Follow the track leading down to the rocky shelf on the foreshore. The plantings of native species along this track are the work of dedicated volunteers who have

Hobart history - Bellerive Oval

Opened in 1914, this became Hobart's first class cricket headquarters in 1987. A significant upgrade was completed in early 2003, including the construction of a new 6000-seat Southern Grandstand. A record crowd of 16,719 witnessed the first game at the newly renovated ground for a one day international between Australia and England. New, huge floodlights suitable for evening games were completed in late 2009.

12 Rosny to Bellerive Beach

Second Bluff

each adopted specific areas. The track curves left around the headland then, just after a concrete boat ramp, heads up towards a footpath on the side of Victoria Esplanade.

7 When you see a wooden rail and steps on your left, carefully cross the esplanade and go up. Follow the track as it winds uphill across a small grassy area until you reach the ditch of Bellerive Fort, built to defend Hobart Town from unwanted invaders.

Walk variations for shorter walks

For a shorter walk, from Bellerive Beach Park, which you reach at waypoint 8, follow instructions for point 11 to return to the start of the walk. An even shorter option is to walk to Bellerive Quay as per points 1-3 then turn left just past the ferry wharf into the main street of Bellerive Village to explore, then go down to the quay and retrace your steps to the start of the walk.

12 Rosny to Bellerive Beach

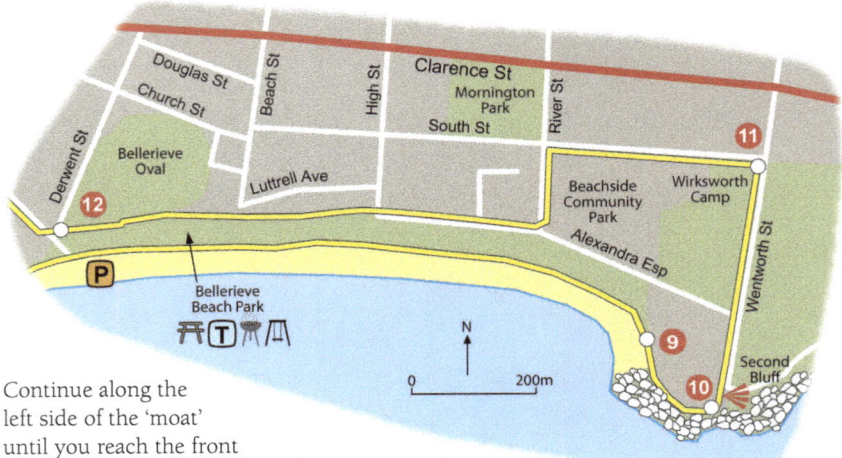

Continue along the left side of the 'moat' until you reach the front entrance to the battery. Here you can take some time to explore.

8 After inspecting the battery, leave via the front entrance, walk through the small car park and along the short driveway then turn right down Gunning Street towards the water. Recross the esplanade to rejoin the Clarence Foreshore Trail, passing a timber deck with steps leading down to the shore. As you approach Bellerive Beach, go down some concrete steps on your right then continue along the beach towards Second Bluff. The beach sand is derived from the local Triassic sandstone and is firm to walk on.

9 A set of steps leads to the top of Second Bluff where a small boulder with a plaque refers to the *Charles Darwin Trail*. Follow the trail and, if you are interested, there are a few narrow tracks that allow you to step out to the edge of the low sandstone cliffs which run along the shore. Take care though, particularly with children, as the drop is steep and unfenced.

10 On the main trail, keep left and walk along a paling fence to exit at the turning circle of Wentworth Street. Turn left and walk down the street, passing Alexandra Esplanade on your left. Pass a sportsground and soon you will reach the impressive buildings of Wirksworth Camp.

11 Turn left into South Street, then left into Lower River Street. You will pass the small Beachside Community Park on your left. Turn right into Alexandra Esplanade, which leads straight onto *Clarence Foreshore Trail*. This meanders between the dunes on the left and suburban back fences

Wirkworth House

12 Rosny to Bellerive Beach

on the right, passes the Bellerive Oval on the right and emerges at Bellerive Beach Park.

12 From the opposite end of the park turn right into Queen Street. You will pass the historic St Marks Chapel of Ease, now a Scout Hall. Walk the full length (three blocks) of Queen Street until you reach Bellerive Village. Here you will find a good bakery/café and some historic buildings such as the old Post and Telegraph Office and the Community Arts Centre. After exploring, head down to the quay and retrace your steps to the start of the walk.

13 Waverley Flora Park

This reserve is situated on top of Mornington Hill and is surrounded by the suburbs of Bellerive and Howrah to the south and Warrane and Mornington to the north. The walk is part of the *Charles Darwin Trail*, the route Darwin is said to have taken while the *HMS Beagle* was on a visit to Hobart in 1836. You will see some beautiful sandstone formations in an old quarry site, pass three lookouts and, in spring and summer, see a wide array of Tasmanian wildflowers, including some rare and endangered species.

Wahlenbergia

At a glance

Grade: Easy/medium
Time: 1 hr
Distance: 2.9 km circuit
Ascent/descent: 100 m / 100 m
Conditions: Well defined track; short steep climb; some steps
More info: Clarence City Council, T 6245 8600, www.ccc.tas.gov.au

Getting there

Car: Take the Tasman Hwy to the Eastern Shore, follow signage to Bellerive; at roundabout turn left into Cambridge Rd then right into Bayfield St which turns into Waverley St after a roundabout; park in the street next to a small playground

Bus: Route 606, stop 19

13 Waverley Flora Park

Walk directions

1 From the upper side of the small playground in Waverley Street a wide gravelled path leads steeply uphill. Pass through the steel gate and walk along a fence. Keep left at a Y-junction to reach the base of an impressive set of stone steps which allow you to rapidly gain great views back over Howrah and Storm Bay.

2 At the top of the steps turn hard left, just before a power pole, and continue along a narrow bush track through Wattles, She-oaks, Native Cherries and Native Hop Bushes. Soon Mt Wellington, with Bellerive in the foreground, will come into view.

3 When you see a long stone wall on your left, and the track begins to curve slightly to the right into a small stand of She-oaks, turn right into a grassy track which soon joins the main central gravel trail through the reserve. Turn right to follow this trail as it snakes along the ridge and then downhill to a junction of six tracks.

4 Go straight ahead; pass under the powerlines and take the next turn to your left only a few metres away. The track leads past some boulders and crosses a watercourse; She-oaks create shelter and shade overhead. Shortly, a historic sandstone quarry face appears on your right. The high quality sandstone from here was used to construct many of Hobart's historic public buildings during the 1800s. The stone was also exported to New Zealand to build the Auckland Post Office. A little further along, after passing the quarry, you will reach a lookout with a low stone wall and a plaque.

5 Turn right to walk along the top of the sandstone cliff face (sometimes used by rock climbers) until you reach a T-junction. Turn left and continue along the well-defined track which leads uphill, ignoring a track coming in on your right, until you see a water reservoir ahead and an aerial on your right.

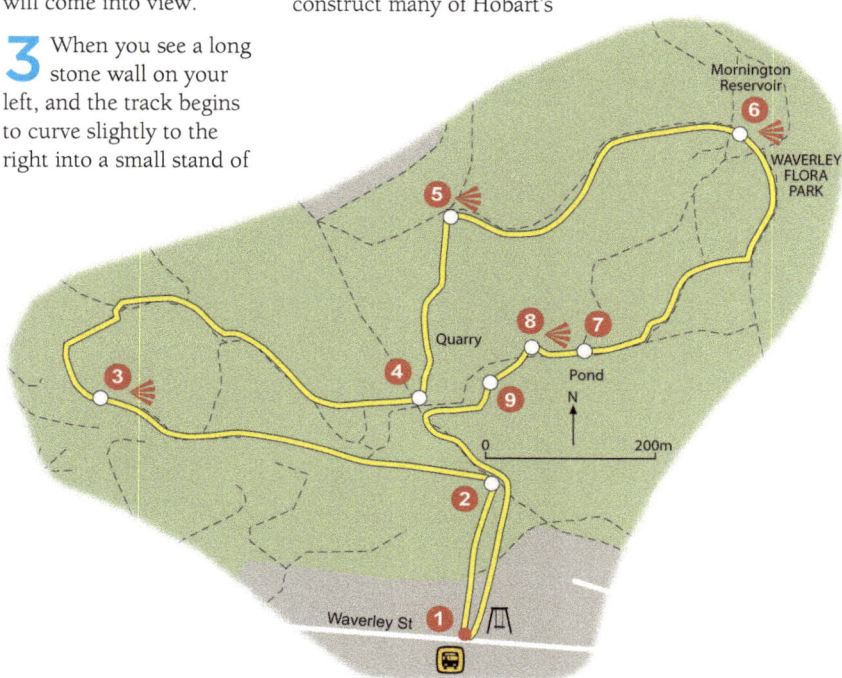

13 Waverley Flora Park

6 Head across some large areas of bedrock, which display an example of 'elephant skin weathering' (which occurs where sandstone has cracked due to impurities of clay within it that have swollen when wet and shrunk when dry), towards the aerial. From here turn right into the main trail which leads downhill in a southwesterly direction.

7 Ignore any side tracks until you come to a Y-junction marked by boulders. A few metres to your left is a small rocky pond which is home to frogs.

8 Continue on the main track and at the next fork make a detour of about 100 metres to the right to a fenced lookout above the historic quarry you passed in point 4.

9 Return to the path, which takes you over another large bedrock area downhill. Follow the main trail back to the 6-way junction, then turn left towards the power pole and the top of the stone steps which will lead you back down to Waverley Street and the start point. On your way down enjoy the view across to Second Bluff which you may have missed on your way up.

13 Waverley Flora Park

Hobart people - Winifred Curtis

The Waverley Flora Park Landcare group describes this park as the 'jewel in the crown' of Hobart's hilltop reserves, due to its exceptionally high biodiversity which has its origin in the variety of the underlying geology and the many microclimates that exist in this area. The park has been used as a teaching site for budding botanists, notably by Winifred Curtis who is well known in Tasmania for the scholarly production of the multi-volumed *Students' Flora of Tasmania*. She lectured in Botany at the University of Tasmania until the mid-1970s using her own works as textbooks. After retirement she helped to establish the Tasmanian Herbarium and continued working in it as an honorary member of staff until 2000, when she was 95. She lived to be a hundred.

14 Calverts Lagoon, Goat Bluff and Calverts Beach

This walk leads you through and past a variety of environments, including a landlocked and brackish lagoon, a tranquil place and a haven for birds (migratory birds from the northern hemisphere can often be observed in this area). The coastal shrub and bushland contains wattles, banksias and small eucalypts. Goat Bluff affords spectacular views across Storm Bay to the Tasman Peninsula and Bruny Island. You can see the much smaller Betsey Island, only about one and a half kilometres away, in the foreground with the infamous Black Jack Rock marked by a light halfway across, and Hope Beach and Cape Direction to the west. Whales can sometimes be spotted from here. Calverts Beach is a popular surfing beach with huge waves pounding the shore, often creating dangerous rip currents.

At a glance

Grade: Easy/medium
Time: 1 hour 25 mins
Distance: 5.5 km circuit
Ascent/descent: 30 m / 30 m
Conditions: Slippery at lagoon, one small climb, exposed in places and a short untracked section; dogs not allowed around the lagoon area
More info: Parks and Wildlife Service, Seven Mile Beach, T 6248 4053

Getting there

Car: Follow the South Arm Hwy to Sandford; about 7 km south of Sandford turn left into Calvert Lagoon Rd (two brown signs at either side of the entrance); park at the end of the road
Bus: Routes 638, 640, 648

Calverts Lagoon

14 Calverts Lagoon, Goat Bluff and Calverts Beach

Walk directions

1 Walk back along the road for about 100 metres until you see a *Calverts Lagoon Conservation Area – walking access only* sign on the right and take the narrow foot track that leads down at first and then to the top of a dune, from where you can see the lagoon. Follow the track down through the reeds - these provide shelter and nesting sites for birds.

2 Walk northwards along the edge of the lagoon – as it's an intermittent wetland the edge can get a bit slippery. If you tread lightly you can expect to see Black Swans, Plovers, Herons, Brown Thornbills and Sea Eagles.

3 As you reach the far side of the lagoon, carefully walk through the reeds to continue along the shore, tending left, and cross the inlet. The shore becomes rocky as you continue in a westerly direction. The South Arm Highway will soon come into view - continue parallel to it until the lagoon's edge curves away from the road.

4 At this stage step onto the grassy area, lined by coastal shrubs, and locate a narrow track which at first runs parallel to the lagoon's shore. A few metres along, make a right turn through the shrubs and soon join a wider track. Turn left at the junction and follow

77

14 Calverts Lagoon, Goat Bluff and Calverts Beach

Calverts Beach

the track through a small grassy area and into the woodland beyond until you reach a large brown sign - *Horses permitted on designated track only* - which is on the Tangara Horse Trail, a network of some 80 kilometres of trails in this area.

5 Turn left into the horse trail and follow it until you reach another brown sign and an interpretive panel about the birdlife and threatened wetland plant species that can be found here, as well as the Calvert Lagoon Road (you have the option to shorten the walk here by turning left and returning to the end of the road and your car).

6 Cross the road to continue on the trail, now becoming quite sandy and a bit braided as it leads through dunes covered with typical coastal vegetation. The easiest way is to keep left. The track emerges at another gravel road.

7 Turn left and head along the road for about 200 metres. Just past 13 boulders and a multi-stemmed Eucalypt turn right, between some more FBRs (as these large traffic-stopping boulders are cheekily nicknamed), into a disused track which swings to the left. After

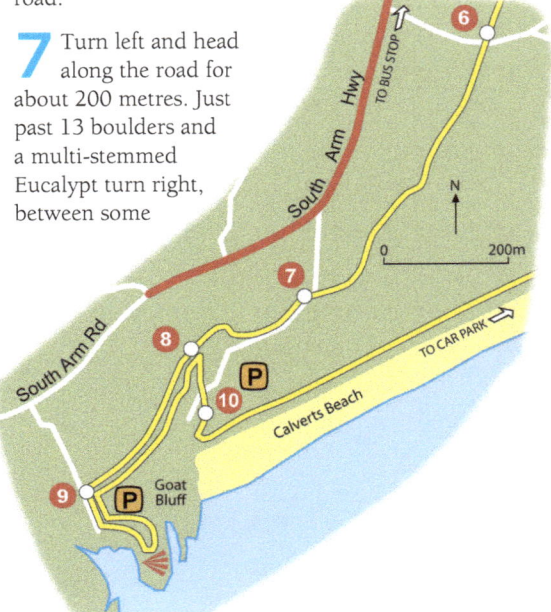

14 Calverts Lagoon, Goat Bluff and Calverts Beach

Hobart environment – the Muttonbird

Muttonbird is the name given to the short-tailed Shearwater, the most abundant Australian seabird. It feeds on krill, squid and fish. Shearwaters are migratory and most of their breeding colonies can be found in Tasmania. Shearwater chicks are raised in underground burrows in sandy, tussocky areas on islands and headlands. They grow very fast and can reach almost twice the weight of an adult. They are the only Australian native bird that is harvested commercially. The industry was established by early European sealers and their Aboriginal families and today forms an important part of Aboriginal culture in Tasmania. Young chicks are taken from their burrows and killed by having their necks wrung. Mutton bird is not something you see on many Tasmanian menus, but they are a delicacy for the Aboriginal community. The cooked bird is very fatty and has a strong fish flavour.

about 50 metres turn left into a narrow foot track by a small white gum that leads off in a southwesterly direction and soon begins to climb up Goat Bluff. To your left is the ocean and a small car park which is used by surfers who frequent Calverts Beach.

8 Continue to climb and keep to the right at a Y-junction. Ignore another track on the left. Near the top of the hill there is a road that leads to Goat Bluff and a brown sign: *South Arm Nature Recreation Area*. Turn left to the lookout and viewing platform to enjoy the panoramic views. While Goat Bluff and Black Jack Reef consist of Permian siltstone, nearby Betsey Island is almost totally made of Jurassic dolerite. A couple of famous vessels ran into problems nearby. The *Hope* was wrecked on

White faced Heron

Hobart history – the *Hope*

The *Hope* was a streamlined barque similar in size to Captain Cook's Endeavour and built for carrying cargo in England in 1793. The ship was apparently bought, very much second hand, by Peter Degraves in 1821, who had it converted to carry fare-paying passengers as well as cargo, thereby increasing its profitability. One stormy night in May 1827 the barque was shipwrecked on the beach which now bears its name. Rumour has it that, among other things, she was carrying gold bullion, but the gold has never been found and the mystery of its whereabouts lives on. Hobart's wide harbour entrance along the Derwent River had hitherto been considered to be one of the safest in the world, but the demise of the Hope caused a review of this belief. As a result Tasmania's first lighthouse was built in 1833 on the Iron Pot, a rock about one kilometres out to sea from Cape Direction at the far end of Hope Beach.

14 Calverts Lagoon, Goat Bluff and Calverts Beach

Goat Bluff

Hope Beach to the west and a large, high speed catamaran was accidentally perched for some time on the southern side of Black Jack Reef in more recent times!

9 Turn back into the foot track that led you here and descend Goat Bluff. Before you lose sight of the small surfer's car park you noted on your way up, carefully pick a route through the grass and bracken fern towards it (if you are worried about any snakes, stomp fairly hard to scare them away, or if you are really worried take the long way around back to the road you crossed,

turn right and walk along it until you reach the little car park).

10 From the car park, walk down to Calverts Beach and turn left to walk along it for about 25 minutes until you see the exit to the Calverts Lagoon car park, about 60 metres before a prominent dune 'tower' and marked by footprints leading in and out.

Walk variation

A rewarding side trip along Hope Beach towards Cape Direction can be made from the Goat Bluff Lookout (point 9 above) by taking the double fenced path to the west which leads down to Hope Beach.

15 Tangara Trail and Gorringes Beach

Coastal scenery, rich flora and birdlife and a beach are the appealing features of this charming coastal walk, part of the 80-kilometre Tangara Trail. Tangara is an Aboriginal word meaning "Let's get away together" a wonderful name for this long network of trails through scenic coastal reserves, undulating semi rural country and small seaside villages on the South Arm Peninsula. It is one of the best recreational trail systems in Australia, constantly growing, and is being used as a model for the establishment of such systems elsewhere.

At a glance

Grade: Easy/medium
Time: 1 hr 40 mins
Distance: 5.9 km circuit
Ascent/descent: 70 m / 70 m
Conditions: Clearly marked trail, rough in sections, with both shady and open sections; shared with horse and bike riders
More info: Clarence City Council T 6245 8600, Parks and Wildlife Service Seven Mile Beach Protected Area, T 6214 8100

Getting there

Car: Take South Arm Rd to Sandford and turn right into Rifle Range Rd which becomes Gellibrand Dr; after 6.8 km from Sandford turn right into a small grassy car park
Bus: Route 644

Tangara Trail

15 Tangara Trail and Gorringes Beach

Walk directions

1 Cross Gellibrand Drive to access the Tanagra Trail to the left of a private driveway and letter box, between some young Blackwoods. The trail is double fenced and follows a power line.

2 Halfway between the first and second power poles turn right into a narrower trail between two sections of post and rails. The trail is also double fenced. The soil here is very sandy and supports Wattles and Bracken Fern. The trail leads past an Emu Farm and gradually turns southeast. The trail passes through a patch of the fine leafed *Melaleuca gibbosa* - which in spring is covered with masses of fluffy, mauve flowers.

3 When you reach a boulder barrier across the track and the end of Kainlani Way on your right, walk through the barrier to continue straight ahead. The bushland becomes denser with White Gums, Black Peppermints and Blue Gums supporting abundant bird life. When you reach a junction with a gravel road. Turn right and walk past a waterhole on the left.

4 Turn right again (back onto the Tangara Trail) just before a steel gate into a private property. After a while the track will begin to rise gently as it winds its way up to the ridge above. In spring you can expect to see the flowers of Black Eyed Susan and Flag Iris. You will pass through a fine stand of Bull Oaks (an upright cousin of the She-oak).

5 As you gain height, the understorey

15 Tangara Trail and Gorringes Beach

Tasmanian Blue Gum flower and operculi

ahead, uphill, where you will find Gellibrand Drive.

6 Cross the road carefully towards O'May Court opposite. Walk down the court; it ends in a turning circle after a curve to the left.

7 Enter another section of the Tangara Trail at the southern end of the turning circle. After a red, white and blue general warning sign for the Mortimer Bay Foreshore, follow the trail downhill until you reach a T-junction. Turn left, then take the next turn to the right to walk along the top edge of the coast. You will pass under beautiful mature Blue Gums with a very healthy understorey of Native Hop Bushes (with their dark green shiny leaves), Daisy Bushes and Correas. There are saggs and tussocks covering the ground and, in spring, a rich array of wildflowers. You will hear Wattlebirds and Honeyeaters in the treetops above and through the trees enjoy views across the River to Mt Wellington.

8 The trail curves around a small bay then goes uphill into a drier area with White Gums and leads along back fences of larger private bush blocks. Gorringes Beach, with its Radiata Pine Tree Plantation, will come into view up ahead.

becomes sparser on the mudstone soils and you will find Silver Peppermint Trees, with their smooth silver trunks and silver grey foliage dominating the canopy. The climb becomes a bit steeper just before you reach a junction of tracks. Go straight

15 Tangara Trail and Gorringes Beach

Walk variation

A nice addition to this walk is to enter the Mortimer Bay Reserve via the signed gate at the car park and follow the sandy track which leads along a narrow plantation of Radiata Pines with Gorringes Beach beyond. The pines have been planted to stabilise the sand, disturbed when mined last century. Sand is an important ingredient in concrete production and is still being mined elsewhere on the peninsula today, although supplies are nearly exhausted. A local Landcare group is caring for this reserve. They have planted hundreds of local native plant species. The area is also used for horse riding which is a popular pastime here. Pass the first *Beach Access* sign and, after about five minutes, turn left at the second *Track* sign for a stroll along the firm sand of this beautiful little beach. You can enjoy views across Ralphs Bay to Opossum Bay and, on the right, Mt Wellington and Hobart's southern suburbs (with the southern ranges far in the background). When you reach the wooden rail fence which protects the bird nesting area, turn left and then right to return to the car park.

15 Tangara Trail and Gorringes Beach

9 Just after the narrow trail turns into a wider vehicular track, turn left to go down to the rocky foreshore where you can see some intricately patterned siltstone paving. Continue along the foreshore vehicular track until you reach a sign telling you that you are entering Mortimer Bay Reserve. This is a sensitive bird breeding area where you'll be able to see Pied and Sooty Oystercatchers, Ducks and Masked Lapwings. Stay on the track until you reach the start point of the walk.

Gorringes Beach, bird breeding area

Hobart environment - Pied Oystercatchers (*Haematopus longirostris*)

Eight pairs studied at Mortimer Bay provided valuable information on breeding success and adult survival. It was found that although the birds can be long-lived, they have a low breeding success due to a small clutch size, a long incubation period, a long interval between hatching and flying and a very high age at first breeding. The protection of their breeding sites is vital for their survival.

16 Arm End

The arm shaped peninsula of South Arm is aptly named. In the crook of the arm is Ralphs Bay, for which a canal development has been controversially proposed and knocked back in recent times. The reserve of 'Arm End', as the name suggests, is the 'thumb and finger' and is a lovely open place to walk. While it appears quite flat from a distance it is in fact undulating and for the keen walker there are a few surprises in store. They include a knoll that allows 360° views, low dolerite sea cliffs, a beach, a sandspit populated by lots of birds and plenty of cultural heritage such as the grave of the original owner of the land and remnants of farming operations. The State Government acquired the land, to protect it from development, from the Calvert family, who had farmed it for years.

At a glance

Grade: Easy/medium
Time: 2 hrs
Distance: 7.25 km circuit
Ascent/descent: 20 m /20 m
Conditions: Exposed, clearly defined but unmarked mown tracks
More info: Clarence City Council, T 6245 8600, www.ccc.tas.gov.au

Getting there

Car: On the Tasman Hwy, turn at Mornington Roundabout into the South Arm Hwy, follow it into Spitfarm Rd and park just north of Opossum Bay
Bus: Route 638, 644, 648

Dolerite outcrop

16 Arm End

Walk directions

1 Enter the signed *Arm End* reserve through a boom gate and turnstile and turn left along the old vehicular track which initially runs along a sandy ditch then curves right to go uphill. Up ahead the magnificent Alum Cliffs appear across the River Derwent; you will also be able to spot the historic Shot Tower just north of the cliffs. The track follows a power line which, after about 20 minutes, ends at a *Broadcast Australia* transmitting station at White Rock Point.

2 From here the track swings to the right and you can see it leading up a small knoll. Ignore a couple of side tracks to the left to climb the knoll for a great lookout and an excellent overview of the area. You will be able to see the continuation of the track northwards.

3 Follow the track as it skirts around the rim of a small depression and then plunges down to meet a wider vehicular track which comes in from Shelley Beach. Continue northwards, with Mary Ann Bay on your left, past some old Macrocarpa pines,

gorse bushes and African Boxthorn (reminders of early European settlement) on your left. Take care if you are walking with children or dogs as these plants are very thorny. This section also has some remnant fencing and rabbit holes, so care is required.

4 Further along a low cliff north of a small beach comes into view. Detour down to the beach via an obvious track then turn left. About 20 metres along you will find the Gellibrand Vault up on the bank; you can pay your respect to William

Gellibrand who rests here - the original grantee at South Arm. This is also a good place to inspect the dolerite outcrop that juts into the sea below the low dolerite cliff.

5 Return to the main track and carefully negotiate the slightly tricky, narrow, eroded section along the top of the cliff

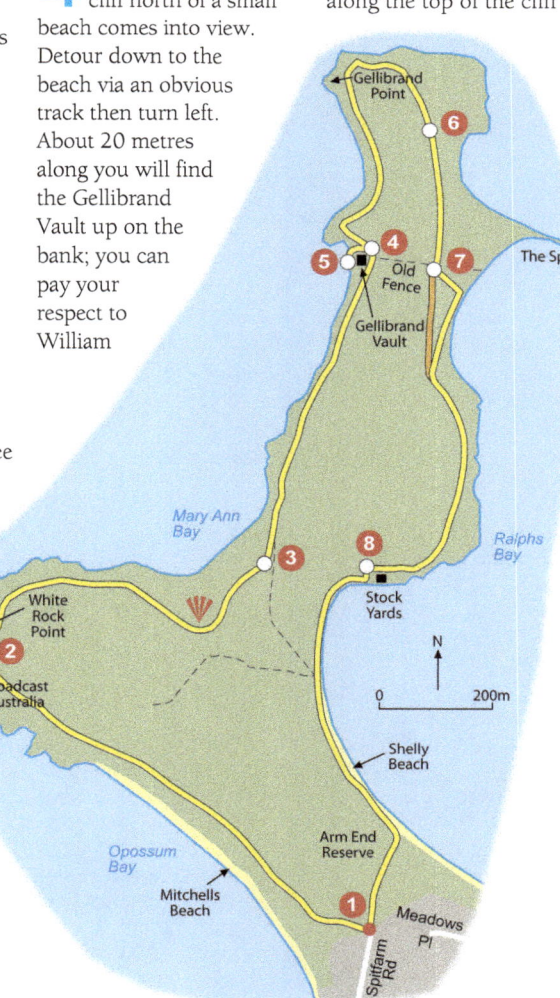

16 Arm End

and past the end of an old fence. The track swings right from here and you will reach the very end of the finger of Arm End. The mown path makes a wide U-turn here to continue southwards and along the other side of the finger.

6 Shortly a pointy sand spit, which reaches into the sea, will appear in view. It is only 50 centimetres above sea level. After passing the spit you will go through an old gateway in a fence.

7 From here you have the option to turn down a track towards the small beach from where you can watch the various birds, such as Pied and Sooty Oystercatchers and Little Pied Cormorants that breed here. Watch the

Hobart people - the Gellibrands

William Gellibrand was granted 2000 acres of land at South Arm in 1824. He lived on his grant and, with the help of twenty convicts, developed it into a farm. This was stocked with horses, cattle, sheep and pigs and a wide range of produce was exported including bacon, hams, sheep skins, bran, oats, barley and hay. Timber and bricks were also sold. Gellibrand often attended meetings in Hobart and was rowed there by boat. William Gellibrand died in Hobart in 1840 and was buried in the vault you can find at the northern end of Mary Ann Bay. His grandson, Thomas Lloyd Gellibrand, inherited the property and lived at Terra Linna. He divided the property into several leaseholds which were later acquired as freeholds.

16 Arm End

birds from a distance that does not make them feel nervous. To continue your walk, locate a narrow foot track that leads south along the top of the bay, just before the gateway onto the beach. Alternatively continue on the mown main track above. Both tracks meet up a little further along.

8 Some old paddock fencing appears not long before you reach some disused stock yards and a loading ramp. The track leads onto the access track for the stock yards, which dips down toward Shelly Beach. At the next Y-junction go down to the beach and walk along it until you come to a post and rail fence that leads into the sea. Turn right to follow the fence up until you reach the start of the walk.

View from Arm End track to Mt Wellington

Hobart environment - African Boxthorn *(Lycium ferocissimum)* and Gorse *(Ulex europaeus)*

Both of these plants have become widely established since introduction into Australia, because they were originally promoted and planted to act as boundary 'fences' between early European properties. These now declared environmental weeds, both hardy, very thorny, fast-growing plants, can seriously affect a property's stock-carrying capacity and also threaten National Parks and Reserves. Both weeds spread particularly well in sandy areas and suppress the growth of grass and herbs, making it easy for rabbits and mice to burrow underneath them - which in turn become a fine food source for feral cats. The thorns of the African Boxthorn can also cause serious injury and pain to people and small grazing animals, and considerable damage to vehicle tyres.

South of Hobart

Two rivers, the North-West Bay River and the Snug River have contributed to the shaping of North-West Bay south of Hobart. The deep bay lies between the headland of Tinderbox Hills to the east and the Snug Tiers to the west.

The first six walks in this chapter will take you to both sides of North-West Bay. Enjoy breathtaking panoramic views from Tinderbox Hills and see both rivers, the North-West Bay River which springs from the top of Mt Wellington and the Snug River which flows from the Snug Tiers. A short foray into the Hartz Mountains, on the edge of Tasmania's wild and beautiful southwest, is included to complete this chapter.

17 Kingston Beach to Boronia Beach

Combine a walk along one of Hobart's most attractive and safe swimming beaches on the shore of the D'Entrecasteaux Channel with a visit to a tiny, secluded beach reserve with impressive sandstone cliffs at the end of a small, shady gully. Boronia Beach is below the site of the historic Boronia Hotel, once a popular destination for day trips from Hobart, though now a private residence. Tall mature Cypress Pines were planted over 100 years ago around the site and you can still see traces of the original terraced garden in the grounds, which were famous for their colourful rhododendrons in spring.

At a glance

Grade: Easy
Time: 1 hr 10 mins
Distance: 3.3 km return
Ascent/descent: 30 m /30 m
Conditions: Beach, narrow foot track and some steps
More info: Kingborough Council, www.kingborough.tas.gov.au

Getting there

Car: From the city take the Southern Outlet to Kingston Beach, turn left into Osbourne Esp and park at the beach's northern end
Bus: Metro routes 67, 68

Southern end of Kingston Beach

17 Kingston Beach to Boronia Beach

Walk directions

1 Walk north of the car parking area, along the esplanade, to Browns River which flows into the D'Entrecasteaux Channel here. Take the footbridge across the river and thence to a picnic area, also a designated dog exercise area. The river here is a popular fishing spot. Then walk along the full length of the beach towards the Kingston Sailing Club building, a boat ramp and a beautiful sandstone cliff.

2 Locate and enter the signed *Boronia Beach Walking Track* which initially leads up a wide, steep bitumen driveway before turning into a narrow foot track that leads along the cliff top. Native Hop bushes, Drooping She-Oaks and Blue Gums grow along the track.

3 You will be able to get a good view of the Channel and the tip of the South Arm Peninsula just before a wooden walkway and access steps from Nicholas Drive. Continue along the track, after a few minutes you will pass another access on the right. Just past a steep, clear grassy area you will come to the gated reserve of Boronia Beach.

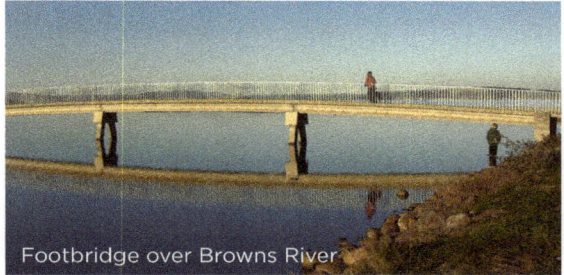

Footbridge over Browns River

17 Kingston Beach to Boronia Beach

4 Enter through the gate and, after rounding the small headland, descend via some stone steps to the tiny beach with its sheltered waters (said to be great for snorkelling). The large conifers provide a shady environment here.

5 Retrace your steps back to the start point.

Kingston Beach

Hobart environment - Tasmania's Floral Emblem

The Tasmanian Blue Gum (*Eucalyptus globulus*) is widespread below 400 metres altitude in the eastern side of Tasmania up to 60 kilometres inland. You will often first notice its presence where you see its distinctive large, crinkly, greyish blue seed capsules and their peaked 'lids' on the forest floor. The tree has rough bark at its base with the top of the trunk a pinkish grey colour. Its adult leaves are up to 30 centimetres long, sickle-shaped and leathery. Juvenile leaves are large, silvery-blue with a red margin and clasp stems in opposite pairs. The Blue Gum is one of the most extensively planted eucalypt due to its rapid growth and adaptability to different environments. In Australia about 65% of hardwood plantations are Blue Gum. Its timber is used for pulpwood, in construction and for fence posts and poles. It is also a primary source of eucalyptus oil production. The tree has been exported as far afield as the Mediterranean (where it grows particularly well), China, Africa, New Zealand and California (where it has become something of a weed!).

17 Kingston Beach to Boronia Beach

Boronia Beach

Hobart environment - Drooping She-Oak

The Drooping She-Oak (*Allocasuarina stricta*) rarely becomes taller than eight metres and often grows on coastal cliff edges in dry, rocky and sunny areas, particularly on dolerite or mudstone soils. It is wind and salt resistant and is said to be one of the most drought tolerant trees in Tasmania.

18 Fossil Cove and Tinderbox Hills

The following two walks can be combined into a day's outing as they are both in close proximity on the Tinderbox Peninsula. Alternatively they can be undertaken separately as very short excursions.

Fossil Cove is a hidden gem only minutes from an outer suburban street and a 'must see' for its interesting rock arch. Tinderbox Hills on the other hand is a walk that leads you along the top of a narrow forested ridge with water views to either side, across Storm Bay to the east and North West Bay to the west. The peninsula contains a few stands of White Gum which are the threatened habitat of the Forty-Spotted Pardalote. They are currently being augmented with plantings by volunteer landcarers.

At a glance

Grade: Easy
Time:
Fossil Cove: 30 mins
Tinderbox Hills: 1½ hrs
Distance:
Fossil Cove: 1 km return
Tinderbox Hills: 3.6 km return
Ascent/descent:
Fossil Cove: 40 m / 40 m
Tinderbox Hills: 70 m / 70 m
Conditions: Steep steps leading down to cove; climb up Tinderbox Hills with short steep sections; mostly shady
More info: Clarence City Council, T 6245 8600, www.ccc.tas.gov.au

18 Fossil Cove and Tinderbox Hills

Finding the tracks

Car: From the city go up Davey Street and turn left into the signed Southern Outlet towards Margate. At the large fork in the road south of Kingston turn left, pass 2 roundabouts and keep left at the next Y-junction to turn into Tinderbox Road East then left into Fossil Cove Drive and park at its end. To continue onto the Tinderbox Hill walk, return to Tinderbox Road East and the Y-junction and take the right arm of the Y, signed Brightwater Road; after about 1 kilometre turn left into Estuary Drive and park at its end.

Walk directions: Tinderbox Hills

1 The track starts at the end of the road and is signposted as a walking and horse riding track. It is initially a gravelled access road to a house.

2 Just before the house there is a Y-junction; keep left to walk along the property boundary until you reach a dog exercise area. There are some beautiful tall Blue Gums here and you will hear and see many birds such as Eastern Rosellas, Little Wattlebirds and Magpies.

3 In a while the track narrows and becomes rockier, with some loose stones. After about ten minutes you will gain enough height for views to the River Derwent and Storm Bay on your left and North West Bay on your right. The main track leads along the ridge top, therefore ignore any minor side tracks which lead onto private property. As the ridge is fairly narrow the views continue in all directions. You will be able to spot South Arm and the Iron Pot light from the end of the track - which is signposted. Nearby you will see evidence of bandicoot activity.

4 Turn back and retrace your steps to enjoy the views you missed earlier because you were facing the other way! The dolerite soils on these hills support a lovely variety of plants and in spring you may find many botanical gems including Native Indigo, Violets, Everlastings and Blue Love Creeper.

18 Fossil Cove and Tinderbox Hills

Walk directions: Fossil Cove

1 Enter the track at the sign *Scenic way to Fossil Cove*. Directly you will come to a large sign interpreting the geology of the area.

2 The track dips down steeply through light bush of Silver and Black Peppermint Gums, Wattles, Heaths and the Tasmanian endemic shrub *Bedfordia linearis* with its silver grey foliage.

3 The track crosses a small gully and leads along a fence on the right.

4 Once you reach the cove you see a natural rock archway on your left with a large rock platform on your right. The rock is Permian mudstone and if you look carefully at the platform you will see a dark band of dolerite which forced its way between the layers of mudstone long ago

View to South Arm

during the Jurassic. At low tide you can quite safely look around both the arch and the platform. The mudstone is finely layered and carries a wealth of fossils. If you enjoy snorkelling, there are some kelp beds along the shoreline to be explored if the weather is fine.

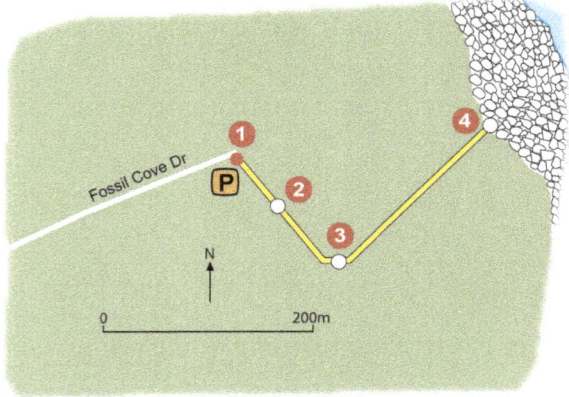

18 Fossil Cove and Tinderbox Hills

Astroloma

Hobart environment – the ancient story of rocks and fossils

During Permian times Tasmania was still joined to the giant supercontinent Gondwana, which, at that time, was situated close to the South Pole. The climate was therefore very cold indeed, but as part of the polar ice sheet melted, sea levels rose and inundated much of Tasmania, filling a shallow depression in its centre. Over around 60 million years or so this depression gradually filled with mud, dead shellfish and other organisms. As icebergs floating above melted, pebbles they had contained were added to the mix. All this weight caused the depression to widen and deepen. You can read some of this story in the Permian mudstone rocks at Fossil Cove.

There's a dark band of dolerite you may find by carefully searching for it in and above the Permian mudstone, and below later mudstones. This band tells the story of the traumatic times that Tasmania experienced during the later Jurassic period. As Gondwana began to split, the earth's crust melted and caused huge amounts of magma to rise from below, pushing the land upwards. In some areas of Tasmania, such as the Central Plateau, this was as much as 600 metres. Where the magma reached flat lying sediments such as the Permian mudstones and Triassic sandstones (laid down after the Permian) it forced its way between the layers. The dinosaurs must have had a hard time as the earth literally moved beneath their feet! Earthquakes were frequent and violent. As the magma cooled in the ground, it formed shrinkage cracks. Subsequent weathering has now exposed these huge amounts of magma - which have become dolerite, the distinctive rock that has given many of Tasmania's mountains their 'organ pipe' looks. The small dark band of dolerite at Fossil Cove is connected to this story.

19 North West Bay River

This short walk through remnant bushland (which has been beautifully restored) leads to a pebble and boulder strewn stream edged by dolerite cliffs. This is one of those delightful places you wish you had discovered earlier. Children from the Margate Primary School have helped to rehabilitate some areas of the native forest, and all children would enjoy this walk especially if you can take some time to explore the streambed with its clear water and river washed pebbles.

At a glance

Grade: Easy
Time: 40 mins
Distance: 1.6 km return
Ascent/descent: 20 m / 20 m
Conditions: Well constructed; shady; short rocky section
More info: Kingborough Council, www.kingborough.tas.gov.au

Getting there

Car: Head up Davey St and turn left into the Southern Outlet; at Kingston turn into Huon Hwy then left into Sandfly Rd; pass the shop and after a dip in the road turn left into the Sandfly Oval to park by a post and rail fence on the left (the signposted start of the track)

19 North West Bay River

Walk directions

1 The track starts off in a northerly direction, parallel to Sandfly Road, for a short distance then curves east to follow Cooke Rivulet downhill. The thick and healthy understorey is full of botanical delights, and depending on the time of year, you can see several rare heath flowers – such as Bushmans Bootlaces and Prickly Beauty - with a canopy of Black Peppermint and Gum-topped Stringy Bark above.

2 As the track goes further towards the river, Native Cherries and Blackwoods appear and then a small clearing on your left with native grasses and some recent plantings of trees and shrubs. A small wooden bridge passes over a natural drain coming in from the right and a set of stone steps leads back up the other side where the canopy changes to White Gums with Wattles and the widespread Tasmanian endemic tall Slender Blanket Leaf shrub (*Bedfordia linearis*) with its distinctive linear, crinkly, two-toned leaves – green on top and light grey 'felt' underside.

3 The track emerges at a small clearing. Turn right to continue along the back fence of a private property (take care with children, the fence has insulators and may be electrified – though I didn't test it to find out!).

4 Turn left towards the river, just before a small clump of Wattles, and you will soon see clear pools of water in between

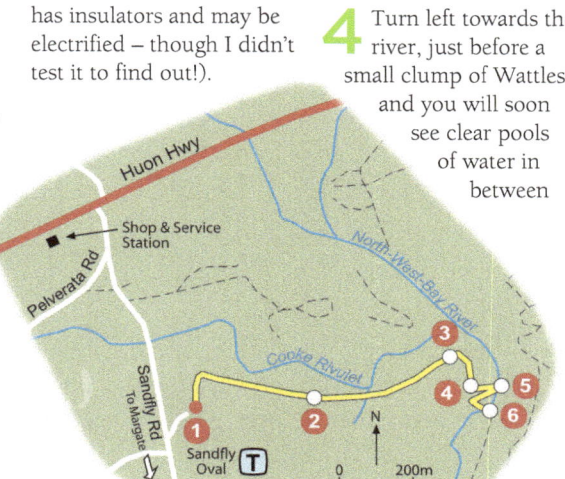

19 North West Bay River

rounded pebbles and boulders - and dolerite cliffs towering above.

5 Return to the fence and follow the now more indistinct track to another clear waterhole beneath the cliffs. Platypus and trout live here – a good spot for a rest and maybe a snack. Children love rock-hopping and exploring the bedrock pools in the river but will need supervision. Pick out dry rocks to walk on, the wet rocks are very slippery.

6 Retrace your steps to the start point.

Hobart environment - Brown Trout

Native to Europe, these were introduced into Tasmania in the 1860s. They can be found in most Tasmanian streams and feed on insects, snails and smaller fish. In autumn and winter adult trout swim upstream in search of suitable gravel beds to spawn. Females prepare small depressions in the gravel to lay their eggs, which are then fertilised by the male fish. Eggs hatch after about one month. As the fish grow they move downstream into deeper water.

19 North West Bay River

Hobart environment – the Platypus

The platypus is the only amphibious, egg-laying mammal in the world. The best time to see this odd animal is early morning or late afternoon. It lives in short burrows just above the waterline of creeks and dams and collects small crustaceans, invertebrates and insect larvae in the mud at the bottom, stores them in its cheek pouches and brings the catch to the surface to eat. In spring it lays, in a long nesting burrow, usually two eggs which hatch in one to two weeks. The young lap up the milk that oozes from the pores in their mother's abdomen and are weaned at about four to five months.

20 Kaoota Tramway Track

This new track was opened in October 2010 and runs along part of an old heritage listed tramway that links Kaoota and Margate. It will take you on a journey back to the time when coal was transported from a mine at Kaoota to the wharf at Margate. This is a lovely relaxing walk, mostly in shade with views across to the Wellington Range. You will cross a couple of creeks along the way to add interest to the walk.

At a glance

Grade: Easy
Time: 3 hrs
Distance: 12 km return
Conditions: Mostly shared (cyclists and horses); gentle gradient
More info: Kingborough Council, www.kingborough.tas.gov.au

Getting there

Car: From Hobart take the Southern Outlet; turn left at Sandfly then right towards Pelverata and Kaoota; follow signs to *Kaoota Tramway Track*; park in the designated spot at the start of the walk

View to Sleeping Beauty

20 Kaoota Tramway Track

Walk directions

1 Initially this track is grassy and descends gently through open bushland with many mature Wattle Trees. Soon it becomes shady and mossy as the vegetation turns into wet sclerophyll and you will see Manferns as you near the first creek crossing.

2 Cross the creek via a wooden bridge. As you climb out of the small gully formed by the creek you will note tall, very aptly named, Cutting Grass (*Gahnia grandis*) plants along the track. They only grow in wet spots and can be a terrible tripping hazard on narrow tracks as well as cause nasty cuts. You will also find Correas here with their bell-shaped red flowers and Guitar Plants (*Lomatia*). The tall gums above are Stringy Bark (*Eucalyptus obliqua*). You may find bits of coal on the track, which have probably fallen out of coal wagons long ago.

3 About half an hour along the track passes a patch of dolerite on the right side. The vegetation changes to dry sclerophyll here. On your left the Wellington Range, with the shape of the 'Sleeping Beauty', can be made out through the sparse vegetation.

4 Further along the track you will find Teatree and Bottlebrushes and pass a house in the bush on your left before descending into another small gully to cross a second creek via a small

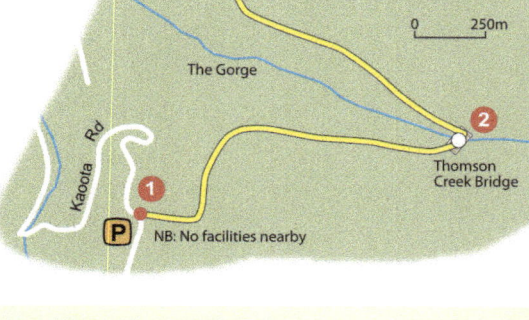

Two-car shuffle

If your party has two vehicles you can arrange to leave one at the finish of the walk.

From the Channel Highway, just before Margate, turn into Sandfly Road and after about 300 metres take the left into Nierinna Road. Follow Nierinna Road for about 2.9 kilometres then turn right into Lawless Road. After passing a poultry farm the road is unsealed and quite narrow. Park your car at the four-way crossroads (limited parking).

20 Kaoota Tramway Track

bridge. Wattles, Blackwoods and some more Cutting Grass can be found here.

5 Soon you will emerge at a four-way crossroads at the end of Lawless Road. Turn back here and retrace your steps to the start point.

20 Kaoota Tramway Track

Hobart history - the Kaoota to Margate tramway

This 2-foot gauge 12½-mile long tramway line was constructed in 1905. It climbed from sea level at Margate Port to 1500 feet at the Kaoota coal mine (which had become the centre of a rapidly expanding coal mining field). However, the line was only used intermittently due to a number of financial collapses among the mining companies involved. The majority of the coal occurred in thin seams and was chiefly extracted using picks and shovels with few mechanical aids.

However, from 1907 to its closure in 1910 the mine was the third highest producer of coal in Tasmania. After the mine's closure, the tramway continued to operate for the public, carrying timber and produce, until in 1915 the government agreed to purchase the tramway. The line was finally pulled up in 1922 and the locomotives sold. Many of the workings were bulldozed in and fenced off, leaving little trace of the industry.

21 Snug Falls

This very popular short walk to picturesque Snug Falls is particularly delightful after some rain. The falls receive their best light from late morning to early afternoon after which time they are in shadow. The water in the shallow pool beneath them is beautifully clear and lovely for a dip on a hot day.

At a glance

Grade: Easy/medium
Time: 50 mins
Distance: 2.1 km return
Descent / Ascent: 80 m / 80 m
Conditions: Well built track; narrow and rocky in places; shady
More info: Kingborough Council, www.kingborough.tas.gov.au

Getting there

Car: From the city head up Davey St and turn left into the Southern Outlet then follow signage to Margate and Snug; from Snug take Snug Tiers Rd next to the brick school building and follow signage to Snug Falls car park (3.6 kms)

21 Snug Falls

Walk directions

1 From the car park, walk up the road about 100 metres and enter the track at a large brown sign on your right - this carries information on track length and walk duration. Initially the track descends in a northerly direction through bushland, on mudstone soil, along the steep banks of the Snug River. The understorey is dominated by Teatree with some Banksias.

2 A little further along, the track follows the contour of the high river bank and crosses a watercourse in a small, mossy gully.

3 After about fifteen minutes you will reach a small shelter shed on a rocky outcrop which serves as a lookout. Continue downwards on the track, as it becomes steeper and rockier, to the left of the shed.

4 Shortly after are some small caves and the butt of a giant Gum tree after which you will catch your first glimpse of the falls tumbling over a spectacular cliff edge.

5 After enjoying this beautiful natural spectacle retrace your steps.

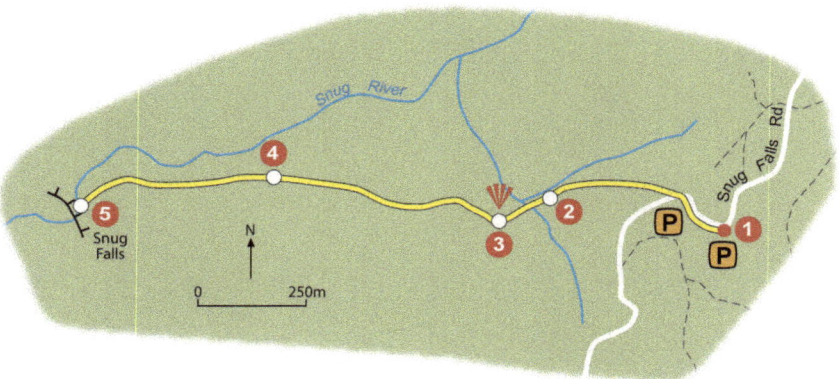

Hobart history - Snug

The French Rear Admiral Bruni D'Entrecasteaux is thought to have been the first European to have sighted this area 1792 as he sailed up the D'Entrecasteaux Channel. The Snug River was discovered and named much later, following the colonisation of Hobart. Subsequent explorations of the Channel coast were undertaken around 1810. This is when the quiet and 'snug' inlet was found and named for this quality.

Settlement followed in the 1830s and 1840s when timber cutters moved in and settlers took up land. The settlers cleared land and used it either for mixed farming or apple and berry orchards. Due to the rugged terrain between Snug and Hobart Town, the main form of transport was ketches and barges along the channel coast. By the 1920s a port and sawmilling facilities were established at nearby North West Bay.

Snug has become urbanised in the last few decades. Being only 30 kilometres south of Hobart it has attracted commuters as well as people interested in alternative lifestyles.

21 Snug Falls

Snug Falls

22 Coningham Reserve

Coningham is a 490-hectare reserve just south of the little village of Snug at the southern end of North West Bay. This circuit route leads through open, grassy woodland and along the top of coastal cliffs - with panoramic views across Snug Bay towards the Wellington Range, Tinderbox and North Bruny Island. Points of interest include a fish farm, sandstone caves and white, sandy beaches. Sea Eagles nest nearby and can often been seen flying overhead. There is some interpretive signage along the way.

At a glance

Grade: Easy/medium
Time: 2½ hrs
Distance: 7.7 km circuit
Ascent/descent: 230 m / 230 m
Conditions: Undulating to steep; strong footwear required; dogs on leash
More info: Kingborough Council, www.kingborough.tas.gov.au

Getting there

Car: About 1 km south of Snug turn left into Old Station Rd, then left into Coningham Rd and right into Hopwood St; park at end of Hopwood St

22 Coningham Reserve

Walk directions

1 The track starts at a brown *Coningham S.R.A.* sign. Follow the vehicle-width grassy track to a weldmesh gate; walk around this and continue across a fire break towards a post which is marked 20 XP. From here continue along the track through some Wild Cherry Trees until you reach a junction with a small track to the left marked by another post. Do NOT turn off but keep to the wider main track, which swings left from here and follows the contour of Sheppards Hill to your left, until you notice another Y-junction.

2 Keep left and begin to climb the hill. Looking back through the sparse, grassy woodland you can enjoy views across Snug Bay towards Snug and, nearer the horizon, the Wellington Range. The bush here was burnt in 2008 and is regenerating well. It is dominated by White Gum (*Eucalyptus viminalis,*), the Tasmanian endemic Blue Gum (*Eucalyptus globulus*) and She-oaks. The trail climbs steeply to a small rocky sandstone outcrop at approximately 160 metres. Some further steep climbing will achieve an elevation of 228 metres where the track levels off. Continue along the top until you reach a T-junction.

3 Turn left onto a rough vehicular track which heads downhill in an easterly direction along the top of a grassy spur towards the coast. When the track becomes steeper, take the foot track that leads off to the right to create a small shortcut towards the end of a gravel road and a turning circle (marked by boulders to bar vehicular access).

4 Continue straight ahead for a short distance until you reach another road. Turn right and follow this to a small car park at its end.

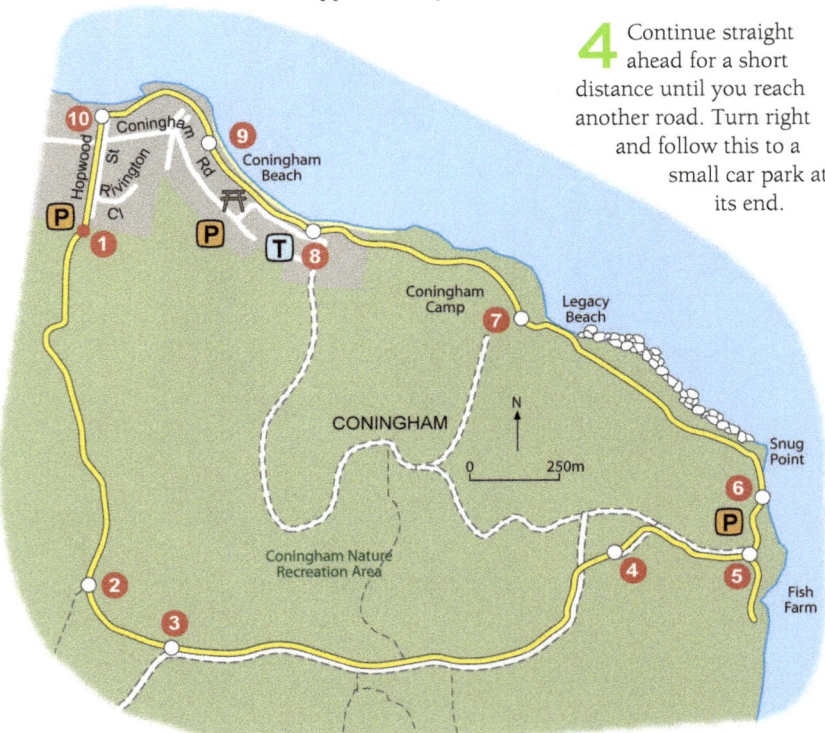

22 Coningham Reserve

5 Take a short side trip from here by turning right into a narrow foot track which leads down to a small bay and a set of steel stairs that go down to water level. A fish farm can be viewed here. Return to the car park and walk along it to find a brown sign: *Coningham Nature Reserve – Cliff top Walking Track*.

6 At a Y-junction, about 30 metres along this track, turn right to a cliff-top fence with a warning sign. A short steep descent, through a narrow gap in the rocks, leads to a cave. This is also a good spot for a snack break with views across to Tinderbox and North Bruny Island (which is less than two kilometres to the east). Return to the Y-junction and turn right to follow

113

22 Coningham Reserve

the well marked cliff-top track until it zigzags down to tiny Legacy Beach, also a lovely spot to rest. You would have passed two sets of interpretive signage, the first about Sea Eagles, Forty Spotted Pardalotes, the eucalyptus Viminalis and Casuarinas and the second about Penguins and Mt Wellington.

7 Leave Legacy Beach and turn right up a wide track with a wooden handrail. At the end of the rail turn right down a narrow foot track. Follow it until you reach a set of six colourful boatsheds on Coningham Beach.

8 Walk the full length of the beach; you will pass a couple of small picnic areas on the left, above the beach.

22 Coningham Reserve

9 Just before another ten boatsheds a set of steps leads up to the foreshore track. Turn right and continue on the track that leads uphill through pleasant coastal vegetation - Boobyallas and Bull Oaks shelter small patches of natural wildflower 'gardens'. In spring you can expect to find Trigger plants and various plants of the heath family amongst the Saggs and Bracken Fern. As the track draws closer to some private backyards, look for a wide weldmesh gate on the left.

10 Turn left to walk around the gate and up a gravel track which will lead you onto Coningham Road. Cross it and continue straight ahead along Hopwood Street until you reach the start point.

Out and about - Tasmania's fish farms

The Atlantic salmon is a member of the family *salmonidae*, which also includes rainbow trout, chinook salmon, brook trout and brown trout. Salmon eggs were originally sourced from a New South Wales hatchery in the early 1980s to begin commercial production of fish. Most fish farms are in the south east of the Huon River, Port Esperance, the Tasman Peninsula area and here in the D'Entrecasteaux Channel. Fish are held in circular floating cages, the largest with a 120 metre circumference and some 15 metres deep. A cage this size contains about 150 tonnes of live salmon. The fish are fed a diet of pellets that contain fish meal (from smaller wild fish), fish oil, grain and milk products, binding agent, plus vitamins and minerals with a pigment added to improve the colour of their flesh. Salmon has become one of the most popular table fish in Australia but some critics describe fish farms as battery hen farms of the sea.

23 Kermandie Falls

This taped route leads upstream through rainforest terrain along the southeastern banks of the beautiful Kermandie River. You will be introduced to many fine examples of Tasmania's rainforest plant species, gain occasional glimpses into the steep river valley and find a particularly picturesque waterfall at the end.

At a glance

Grade: Medium
Time: 2 hrs
Distance: 5 km return
Ascent/descent: 240 m / 240 m
Conditions: Can be wet, muddy and slippery at times; some bushwalking experience is needed to follow the tapes, especially around fallen trees, it is recommended that you walk in a party and do not proceed if you think you may have missed any tape or marker

Getting there

Car: Take the Huon Hwy to Geeveston and turn right into Arve Rd, towards the Tahune Air Walk; after about 6.2 km turn left into an unmarked forestry road (Oigles Rd) and follow it for about 4.3 km to a bridge over the Kermandie River; the signed track entrance is just across the bridge

23 Kermandie Falls

Walk directions

1 Initially the track leads to the top of a road cutting. Keep right and follow an old fern-lined 4WD track which ends at the river.

2 Locate a rough foot track to your left, which is marked with pink tape and rises up the river bank. The clumps of tall grasses seen here are sharp-edged Cutting Grass (*Gahnia grandis*), well known as a tripping hazard for bushwalkers.

3 Shortly you will pass a small concrete weir in the river and, a little later, cross a tributary. The track marker tapes vary in colour from pink to the less visible yellow with the occasional fluro orange paint spot on logs or rocks. After another weir, the track veers away a little from the river for a short distance. However, the river remains within earshot for the entire walk.

4 There are tall gums towering overhead as well as Sassafras, Myrtle, Celery Top Pine and Blackwood. These are generally known as minor species of timber and sought after by artisans and furniture makers. Manferns and Cutting Grass line the track as it traverses a boggy area.

5 Look out for the huge Eucalypt stumps that were left behind by timber cutters last century. Just past a particularly large stump to your right, the track rises higher up on the river bank and you reach a small lookout to the river.

6 Continue along the route as you stumble over fallen branches under giant gum trees. The track soon leads along the base of a small rocky outcrop on your left. Shortly you will see a giant grandfather Myrtle Tree on your right, spreading its moss and fern covered arms over the track.

7 The path plunges into a cool and shady forest of ancient, tall Manferns and you might find yourself looking out for a troll or goblin to emerge from underneath one of the mossy logs across the

Walk variation

A shorter walk to Kermandie Falls (1.5 km return, 1 hr) can be begun from the end of Riawunna Road. Continue along the Huon Highway through Geeveston for about 4 km then turn right into Hermons Road. After passing the rubbish tip, keep right at a Y-junction then turn right into Riawunna Road. After about 10 km from the Huon Highway turn-off, park your car in the designated parking area.

23 Kermandie Falls

track. You will soon be able to catch another glimpse of the river and the rapids in it, before the track rises steeply along the top of the river bank over clay soils and tree roots. At this stage the track acquires a distinct 'yo-yo' quality as it makes its way along the river. Take care not to lose sight of the marker tapes. You will pass another more open section, with views downstream, then pass round the end of a large log on your right to follow the river bank more closely. There are occasional views to the opposite river bank as the valley becomes narrower and steeper.

8 You will experience a brief encounter with the endemic Horizontal Scrub - which has made life difficult for bush pioneers through its growth habit.

23 Kermandie Falls

Initial shoots form tall and slender trunks which fall over then sprout slender upwards shoots along the fallen trunk which then fall over to sprout upwards shoots etc etc..... eventually creating an impenetrable thicket.

9 The track now sidles along the ever-narrowing river valley as you near the falls. One last 'hurdle', at the time of writing, is a huge rotten tree which has fallen across the track to the river's edge and shattered completely in the process. You will find it easiest to go up a few steps to the left and look for the obvious 'detour' created by walkers that went before.

10 Next you will come to a signed track junction where an alternative route comes in from the left. Continue straight ahead along a final steep section before descending along the foot of a dripping dolerite cliff towards the base to Kermandie Falls.

11 This is a lovely spot for a rest before you retrace your steps to the start point.

Hobart environment - important minor timber species

Blackwood (Acacia melanoxylon) is a beautiful, satiny, golden-brown to dark brown colour, with a reddish tint and streaks and shows distinct growth rings. Its grain can be straight or wavy. It is considered to be one of the most decorative of Australian timbers. It is used for sliced veneer, cabinet work and furniture.

Sassafas (*Atherosperma moschatum*)

This timber is pale grey to light brown with blackish streaks (thought to be caused by a fungus). It is fine and straight grained and very attractive. It is easy to work and used for joinery and specialty work.

Myrtle (*Nothofagus cunninghamii*)

Distinctive pinkish to red-brown colour, fine texture and straight or slightly interlocked grain. A beautiful smooth timber for furniture and cabinet production.

Celery Top Pine (*Phyllocladus aspleniifolius*)

Is an unusual endemic Tasmanian conifer with needles that look like celery leaves. Its wood is creamy or fawn coloured and growth rings are easily seen. This is a hard and strong timber with low shrinkage that bends and works well. It is also very durable and has been used for railway sleepers, strainer posts, in boat building and as truck and house flooring as well as in joinery.

Gift shops and markets such as Salamanca Market (see walk No 1) usually offer objects made from these timbers for sale.

24 Hartz Peak

The Hartz Mountains have been a popular bushwalking destination since the early 1900s and continue to attract keen walkers of all ages. The area, which covers 7250 hectares, was set aside as a scenic reserve in 1939 and proclaimed a national park in 1959, before finally being included in the World Heritage Area in 1989 to preserve its significant natural and cultural heritage.

The most distinctive feature of the park is the Devils Backbone, a dolerite mountain range that runs north-south and is terminated by Hartz Peak and Mt Snowy at the southern end. This walk will take you along the eastern, glacier-shaped plateau at the base of the backbone, then up to Hartz Pass. The track then continues south atop the 'backbone' and ends in the final climb up to the peak.

At a glance

Grade: Medium/hard
Time: 4.5 hrs
Distance: 12.5 km return
Ascent/descent: 400 m / 400 m
Conditions: Rocky sections, some steep with some rock hopping near the summit; very exposed with high rainfall; strong footwear and full kit are essential; check the weather forecast
More info: www.parks.tas.gov.au, Hartz Mountains National Park, T 6264 8460

Getting there

Car: From Hobart take the Huon Hwy to Geeveston, then turn right into Arve Rd and follow signage to Hartz Mountains NP, ignoring all logging spurs; park at the end of the road (about 84 km from Hobart)

24 Hartz Peak

Walk directions

1 From the parking area head for the large modern shelter building, at the southern side of the turning circle. This contains a walker registration box, tables and seating, water tap and interpretive panels giving an overview of the park's features and its history. The Hartz Peak track starts along the western side of the shelter.

2 After crossing and recrossing a tributary of the Arve River along some duck-boarding and, only about five minutes along the track, you will pass the memorial plaque to Arthur and Sidney Geeves who perished from exhaustion and hypothermia near here in 1897.

3 Typical sub-alpine vegetation lines the track as it rises gently along the narrow plateau that has been shaped by a small glacier during the last few ice ages. In the wet areas you will find Cutting Grass, Bauera, Tea tree and two tufty Tasmanian endemics belonging to the lily family of plants: Pineapple Grass (aptly named as it resembles pineapple tops) and a larger version known as *Milligania densiflora*. During November or December you may also be able to spot the beautiful, red Tasmanian Waratah, a dainty cousin of the NSW variety. The canopy here is dominated by the Tasmanian Snow Gum.

4 As you gain enough height to reach the tree line the dolerite range known as Devils Backbone which borders the plateau appears on your right. Numerous small tarns have formed in depressions created by glaciation. The area is quite similar to the equally popular Tarn Shelf in the Mt Field National Park (see Walk 35). The vegetation becomes dominated by alpine heath plants, sedges and ferns. The abundant lacy fern you can see carpeting the ground around the small tarns is Scrambling Coral Fern (*Gleichenia microphylla*).

24 Hartz Peak

5 When you arrive at the cord-wooded turn-off to Lake Esperance, take this side trip of only a couple of hundred metres as it is well worth the effort. There is a well appointed resting spot by the cool, clear waters of the lake and some interpretive panels about the bright green alpine cushion plants you would have noticed along the track by now. Across the lake you may be able to spot a small stand of King Billy Pines (*Athrotaxis selaginoides*).

6 Return to the main track to continue along the tarn shelf. The dome shaped mountains you can see up ahead now are Mt Snowy on the left and Hartz Peak, your destination, to the right. On clear days you can see eastwards as far as the Huon Estuary, the D'Entrecasteaux Channel and Bruny Island.

Cushion plant

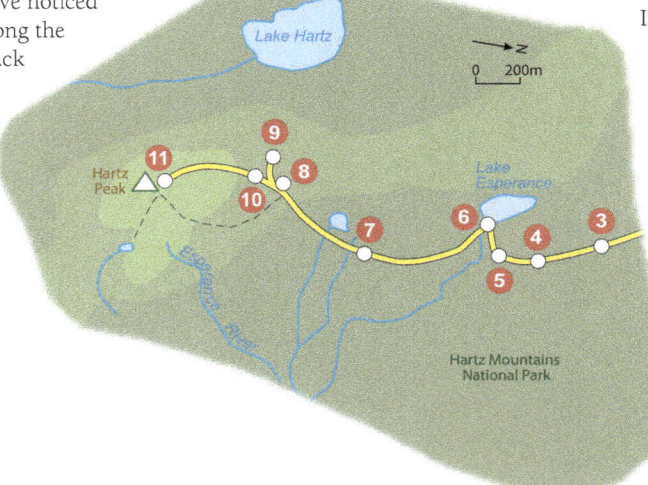

24 Hartz Peak

Hartz Lake

7 The track continues to rise to a slightly higher level of the plateau, which holds a number of larger tarns. A signposted 'paved' track on your right leads to Ladies Tarn about fifty metres away and also worth a quick visit.

8 Next a short, very steep climb will lead you up to Hartz Pass. At the top there is a sign pointing to Hartz Peak on the left.

9 However, for a closer and more personal look at Hartz Lake and the particularly well formed, photogenic, terminal glacial moraine that dams the lake, continue straight ahead. This is a much fainter track that is sparsely cairned and marked with stakes. Continue on it in a westerly direction for about 250 metres until you reach a small rocky outcrop just before a steep plunge into the dense and prickly shrubbery below. This is a lovely vantage point for a short rest. It's interesting to imagine how the glacier crept along the plateau, picking up rocks and bulldozing them along until finally dropping them to form the dam when it melted.

10 Return to the main track and turn right to walk along the spur that leads to the steep final ascent. Here you will begin to see the large pieces of shattered dolerite that cap the mountain. A bit of rock-hopping between cairns is necessary to reach the summit.

11 On a clear day you are rewarded with 360° views and a wonderful snapshot introduction to Tasmania's south western wilderness. To the south you can see Precipitous Bluff, to the west Mt Bobs and Federation Peak and further northwards the South Picton Range and Mt Picton.

12 Retrace your steps to the car park and note how different the views of the landscape are on your way back!

24 Hartz Peak

Hartz Peak

Hobart environment - Lake Osbourne,

Accessible from the northern end of the car park, this lake is only a 40 minute return walk away, and if you have the time and energy you can visit it on the same day as Hartz Peak. There are some particularly good interpretive panels along the way. The track initially leads through a 'tunnel' of stunted rainforest species, before some duckboarding takes you over some sedgeland to the lake's shore, where you can see a small specimen of King Billy Pine.

Hobart environment - King Billy Pine (*Athrotaxis selaginoides*)

This endemic Tasmanian conifer grows at altitudes above 600 metres and can reach heights of 40 metres. It is slow growing and can reach ages of over 1200 years. Its durable, pinkish timber is easy to work and sought after for boat building and craftwood. Many old Tasmanian homes have window frames and sashes made from King Billy Pine. Sadly, large numbers of King Billy Pines have been destroyed by fire in the past, their mournful white skeletons can often be seen in the Tasmanian mountain landscape. They are extremely slow to regenerate. Part of the Parks management strategy is to eliminate all fires, where possible, to prevent further loss of this precious conifer and many other slow growing alpine plants as well.

24 Hartz Peak

'The Mountain'

Hobartians look up to Mt Wellington's rugged and wild beauty, with its distinctive dolerite 'organ pipes', and are proud to call it their own. Since first settlement , the mountain's numerous springs have provided abundant, clear drinking water. It is thought that George Bass was the first European man to climb it in 1798. Since then famous botanists such as Robert Brown, belonging to Collins' settlement party, and Alan Cunningham have collected plant specimens from the rich flora, which to this day comprises well over three hundred species, many of them endemic to Tasmania. Charles Darwin reached the top in 1836 and Lady Jane Franklin was probably the first European woman to climb it in 1837.

The mountain soon became a favourite 'playground'. From the 1880s people began to build rustic huts as week-end retreats in secluded bush locations on the lower slopes, though, alas, most of these were lost in the 1967 bushfires. A network of tracks was constructed during the early 1900s, some of which are included here.

Weather conditions on Mt Wellington can change rapidly; make sure you read the notes in the introduction under 'Be Prepared' and 'Navigation' in this guide before setting off. Generally summit temperatures are eight to ten degrees colder than in Hobart City.

Mt Wellington Plateau

25 Fern Tree, Silver Falls and Dunns Creek

Explore the lush vegetation of the Browns River and Dunns Creek gullies in the shady, southeastern slopes of Mt Welllington. This area is much loved by locals and tourists alike and there is a network of tracks and trails inviting you to find new variations to this circuit; a great introductory walk.

Silver Falls

At a glance

Grade: Easy/medium
Time: 1.1 hrs
Distance: 2.8 km circuit
Ascent/descent: 260 m / 260 m
Conditions: Well constructed tracks with short, steep, rocky section; shady
More info: Wellington Park Management Trust T 6238 2176, Hobart City Council Infoline T 6278 0200

Getting there

Car: From the city drive up Davey St keeping to the right to avoid a forced left turn down the Southern Outlet; keep straight ahead along Davey St as it becomes Huon Rd; park in a car park on the right just 50 m past the turn off to the summit

Bus: Routes 48/49 to Fern Tree Tavern then walk back down the road to the car park as above

25 Fern Tree, Silver Falls and Dunns Creek

Walk directions

1 The track starts on the eastern side of the car park to the left of a small waterfall in Dunns Creek. It is well signposted and rises steeply alongside the creek via some stone steps.

2 After only a few metres, just before a bridge over the creek, take a left turn onto the track marked *Fern Tree Bower Reserve*. This track switches back towards the Huon Road and heads along above it, passing the small, historic, wooden church that survived the terrible bushfires in 1967. Shortly you'll emerge in Fern Tree Park, a delightful, shady picnic area under very tall gum trees, planted with man ferns and rhododendrons; an exotic garden plant that does particularly well in this mountain climate.

3 Locate the stone picnic shelter at the far end of the park and head left down towards the road, then turn right into the wide, shared path signposted *Pipeline Track*. It leads off parallel to the old Huon Road. Pass another picnic shelter with BBQ facilities. Underfoot you may be able to spot some evidence of the pipeline, in the form of stone slabs, which continues on to the Waterworks Reserve (see Walk 8) from here. There are also a couple

Fern Tree Park

129

25 Fern Tree, Silver Falls and Dunns Creek

of interesting old park benches along the way.

4 Tall Tasmanian Blue Gums now form the canopy overhead. The forest is wet sclerophyll and there are some fine leafed Myrtles growing here as well. The track veers away from the road after a few minutes and you will hear the rushing of Browns River in the fern-filled gully below on your left. Pass a concrete valve housing to come to the Fern Tree Bower, a small clearing and track junction furnished with an interpretive sign about the waterworks on your left and an historic stone monument on your right. A few metres along the Pipeline Track, which

leads off to the left, you can also find one of the old shelters and picnics huts and a panel outlining the history of the Ferntree Bower.

5 However, continue straight ahead along the signed *Silver Falls Track*. This rises gently and, after a few minutes, the falls tumbling over a mudstone shelf with a viewing platform and bridge crossing the river in front of them come into view. The water running down the river from here is the 'environmental flow'. Any surplus is being diverted into a pipe above the falls and contributes to Hobart's water supply.

6 Cross the bridge; the track now rises steeply via another set of fenced stone steps and becomes rockier.

25 Fern Tree, Silver Falls and Dunns Creek

The Springs

7 Turn left after only a few metres into *Reids Track*, which eventually leads to the Springs. This short section of the walk is quite steep (you will gain over 100 metres in elevation), narrow, rocky and can be slippery in wet conditions. Ignore a vehicle service track that crosses (no public access) and continue straight ahead. Pass a patch of tall Cutting Grass and, soon after, reach the Triassic sandstone layer that overlays the Permian mudstone. The tall heath-like plant you can see here along the track is a Tasmanian endemic, *Richea dracophylla*, which is related to the giant Pandani plants that stand in the alpine landscape like families of people (see description of the Lake Dobson Circuit, walk no. 34).

8 At the next junction turn left and follow the *Radfords Track*, which rises gently, uphill until you reach the Springs picnic and parking area.

Hobart environment - *Richea dracophylla*

Richea dracophylla literally means 'dragon-leafed richea'. It belongs to the Heath family and is endemic to Tasmania. A tall straggly plant (up to three metres) with long, pointy-bladed leaves arranged in a spiral around the stem, it looks quite 'architectural'. Creamy white flower spikes with distinctive brown bracts appear in spring. Richea dracophylla is rarely grown in gardens as it is not very adaptable to climates other than its natural habitat of wet forests.

25 Fern Tree, Silver Falls and Dunns Creek

9 This is the highest point of this walk (about 680 m), and a good spot for a rest before returning to *Radfords Track* and the junction with *Reids Track*.

10 This time go straight ahead and enjoy the gentle downhill slope on this wider track, which is edged with Hard Water-ferns. Ignore *Middle Track* coming in from the right. Soon you'll spot Radfords Monument, on your left at a track junction, a memorial to a young runner who perished here.

11 Turn right into *Fern Glade Track*, which zigzags all the way downhill to the Huon Road and your car, crossing and re-crossing Dunns Creek no less than eleven times. This section of your walk has a stand of tall Silver Wattles and Man Ferns that increase in height in search of light, as you move downhill. During spring and summer you may hear the trilling song of a fan-tailed cuckoo. Many different birds can be heard in this delightful area.

Hard Water fern

Fern Tree Bower

25 Fern Tree, Silver Falls and Dunns Creek

Hobart history - Fern Tree and the 1967 fires

The 1967 bushfires in southeastern Tasmania were the most destructive fires experienced in Australia to that date, with the possible exception of the Victorian fires of 1939, and had a comparable impact to the more recent holocausts in South Australia and Victoria. One hundred and ten separate fires created an inferno of unbelievable proportions across the region. Many areas were totally devastated. Fern Tree lost eighty per cent of its houses plus its two-storey timber Springs Hotel, (the foundations can still be seen opposite the Springs, at the start of Walk 26), the shop and parish hall (when a fire originating from Tolosa Park to the north crossed the Strickland Avenue-Huon Road junction and burnt towards Bracken Lane). About two hundred people, who tried to shelter in front of the Fern Tree Hotel, had to be evacuated by trucks sent up from Hobart. Luckily no lives were lost at Fern Tree on this terrible day; however the fires cost 62 lives in other areas and over 1,300 homes were destroyed, some only a kilometre from Hobart's CBD.

26 Zig Zag Track, Summit and Icehouses

In fine weather this walk promises you breathtaking views of Hobart and its environs. You will also pass through some beautiful vegetation communities and have the chance to see Mt Wellington's dolerite cap, with its natural rock sculptures, up close.

At a glance

Grade: Medium/hard
Time: 4 hrs
Distance: 7 km circuit
Ascent/descent: 550 m / 550 m
Conditions: Start to summit well built and defined, steep, rocky track; return less defined, cairned route for experienced walkers
More info: Wellington Park Management Trust T 6238 2176, Hobart City Council Infoline T 6278 0200

Getting there

Car: From the city drive up Davey St keeping to the right to avoid a forced left turn down the Southern Outlet; keep straight ahead as Davey becomes Huon Road; follow signage to Mt Wellington; at The Springs turn left into the loop road and park at the top just past the old Springs Hotel site

26 Zig Zag Track, Summit and Icehouses

Walk directions

1 The track begins at a signposted set of stone steps which lead up through tall wet sclerophyll forest understorey. Pass a fenced UTAS Cosmic Ray Observatory on your right and, after a few minutes, you'll reach a small clearing and track junction.

2 Go straight ahead on the signed *Pinnacle Track*, which leads through the dense understorey and follows some rusty pipes. The gradient becomes less steep as you cross several watercourses and pass a small waterfall on your left. The track is lined with tall shrubs such as Dragon Heath, Hakea and Blanket Bush, which in spring often have very showy flowers. Cutting Grass grows in the wet spots.

3 As you cross a boulder field you may hear Whistlers, Black Cockatoos

Pinnacle Track

26 Zig Zag Track, Summit and Icehouses

and Black Currawongs in the trees above and you'll soon see panoramic views down to Hobart.

4 You'll pass a small cenotaph plaque, placed by the Hobart Walking Club in memory of Joseph Mark Richards, who died while competing in the 'Go as you Please' race to the pinnacle in 1903. The vegetation now includes Pepperberries and Snowberries and the track becomes steeper just before the junction with the *Zig Zag Track*.

5 At this junction there is a rustic wooden seat that lends itself to a cuppa (if you've brought a flask) and a rest before the steeper ascent towards the summit plateau. Turn left onto the *Zig Zag Track* to continue your walk through thinning vegetation. In November and December you will see the beautiful red Tasmanian Waratah flowering in profusion. You will also see alpine plants, such as pineapple grass growing along the track. The Snow Gums above become sparser and lower as you approach the tree line. Soon you'll catch your first sight of the Organ Pipes, the summit ahead and sweeping views of the city below.

6 The top part of the track is particularly well built with sections of stabilising stone walling, stone steps and guide posts with connecting chains. A small lookout with stone seating is another good place to rest before the final assault to the summit - where it is mostly cold and windy.

26 Zig Zag Track, Summit and Icehouses

7 As you reach the top, the track becomes gravelled. Walk towards the large TV tower (which is visible from the city below), until you come to a junction with the signed *South Wellington Track* that switches back to your left.

8 Turn left and follow this much less defined track. Bright orange markers on posts show the way. Be sure to only proceed when you see the next marker, especially in 'white out' conditions, which can occur any time. The track leads across alpine heathland that is strewn with well-weathered dolerite tors and boulders of truly sculptural quality - and on a clear day the views all around are exhilarating, a wonderful

Zig Zag Track

26 Zig Zag Track, Summit and Icehouses

reward for the climb. The route leads along the eastern edge of the plateau and descends gently at first.

9 After a wet and boggy area, cross a small rise before a steeper descent past a number of small tarns. An old wooden sign to the left, indicating Rocking Stone, leads (if you have the time) to a fine lookout, interesting balancing stone feature - a great spot for a picnic. The route is marked with old yellow markers and stone cairns.

10 Continue downhill on the main track, which increases in steepness as you work your way along the base, and through some large boulders before reaching the treeline and a junction with the track to Smiths Monument (45 minutes away).

Ice House Track

Hobart history - Ice Houses

Built from the 1850s, using convict labour, these box-like structures were about seven metres square, with thick stone walls and brushwood roofs. Frozen snow was rammed into them to make ice, which was later cut out in blocks, wrapped in blankets and taken out by packhorse along a purpose built bridle path. The ice was used in hospitals and anywhere else where ice was needed. It is reported in the daily newspaper in 1885 that *"citizens are delighted at a trifling cost with a luxury only properly appreciated by the panting polka dancer, or by the restless fever patient whose temples are cooled by the delicious application of the Ice"*. Alas, the foundations are now all that remain.

26 Zig Zag Track, Summit and Icehouses

11 Keep on the *Ice House Track*, which curves to the left here. The track markers change to yellow and orange, occasionally on trees (the Snow Gum woodland becomes denser and taller and there is a lot of lichen and moss). The track follows the contour for a while and passes a post with a sign informing you that you can find the ruins of one of the ice houses in the bush about 20 metres to your right.

12 After exploring the site, continue downhill past a large boulder field on your left. Shortly the track curves to your right to follow the contour, then dips down steeply. Take care as the rocks here can be slippery. There are less markers, but the track is well trodden.

You'll pass a wet section of mixed wet forest with Native Fuchsia, Bauera, Hakea and Dragon Bush in the understorey.

13 At the junction with gravelled *Milles Track*, turn left and enjoy the lovely vistas down to the Tasman Bridge, CBD, Eastern Shore, South Arm and Bruny Island (with Ridgeway in the foreground). Ignore a track coming in from the right and continue until you reach the small clearing and track junction you crossed at the beginning of your walk. Turn right and retrace your steps back to your starting point.

Hobart environment - Tasmanian Waratah

This shrub (*Telopea truncata*) is commonly about three metres tall with bright red flowers that are somewhat daintier than their mainland cousins. These plants prefer wet sclerophyll forest or subalpine scrubland at altitudes from 600 to 1200 metres. The best time to see them flowering is in November and December.

27 St Crispins Well

Cathedral Rock (880 metres above sea level), part of the Wellington Range, stands out in the landscape south of Hobart due to its distinctive shape. It overlooks the valley cut by the North West Bay River and you will be able to see across to it during this scenic walk. St Crispins Well is part of the original water supply system to Hobart (see Walk 8) and still operates today.

Pipeline track

At a glance

Grade: Easy
Time: 3 hrs
Distance: 10.5 km return
Ascent/descent: 100 m / 100 m
Conditions: Easy walk on wide old vehicular track, mostly shady
More info: Wellington Park Management Trust T 6238 2176, Hobart City Council Infoline T 6278 0200

Getting there

Car: From the city drive up Davey St keeping to the right to avoid a forced left turn down the Southern Outlet; keep straight as it becomes Huon Road; 3 km after passing Fern Tree Tavern park in a car park at the Morphetts Rd turnoff on the left

27 St Crispins Well

Walk directions

1 Carefully cross the road towards the start of the walk (signposted to the *Pipeline Track* and shared with bikes). The track leads uphill for a short way, then levels off. After a few minutes you will come to the *Pipeline Track* junction.

2 Turn left, along the contour of the lower slopes of Mt Wellington. The bush is wet sclerophyll strewn with large dolerite boulders and contains species that thrive in higher rainfall, such as Blanket Bush and Man Ferns.

3 After about 20 minutes, cross a small stream where, in spring, you can find the beautiful, white starry flowers of Clematis. From here you can see across the valley to Leslie Vale with The Channel in the distance. Snowberries and Cutting Grass grow among the moss-covered rocks and you can hear many birds overhead, especially the black

27 St Crispins Well

currawong. Further along, in another 40 minutes or so, there are some warning signs for bikes to slow down around the blind bends - the track winds in and out of small gullies created by watercourses.

4 On your left you will be able to spot some sections of the old pipeline in the bush below, before you reach a turn-off to Snake Plains.

5 Continue along the *Pipeline Track*. In about 50 metres head through a gate, which is the boundary of Wellington Park and the water catchment area. On your left appears the magnificent and distinctive Cathedral Rock. Not far from here a well-built dry stone wall supports the track.

6 Ignore a side track, by a pressure release valve in the pipeline, leading steeply downhill (it leads down to the North West Bay River which has cut this deep valley). The bush becomes drier here on the mudstone soils as the track continues to wind along the contours, passing a *no access* road.

7 Soon the track crosses a large rock scree and another *no access* track before arriving at a small tin hut. This contains a fire place and a bench seat - most welcome in wet weather.

27 St Crispins Well

8 Take the short narrow track, which leads uphill across the road from the hut, to St Crispins Well. Take care with young children as there is a steep drop down to the road. The well is only a few minutes away in a shady glade and has a fenced viewing platform with a seat. A small waterfall tumbles into the funnel shaped stone dam from which some of the water is piped to Hobart. This is a pleasant spot for a picnic or snack.

9 Retrace your steps to the start point, taking care when crossing the road back to your car.

St Crispins Well

28 Collins Bonnet

Most of the height for this walk along the top of the Wellington Range is gained by driving your car up to the 1100 metre level before setting off. If you pick a clear day you will be able to enjoy far ranging views across the northern suburbs of Hobart and south into the Mountain River Valley as far as Franklin in the Huon. The vegetation along the track is varied, interesting and, in summer, reminiscent of walking through a well-planted rock garden.

Summit and view into Mountain River

At a glance

Grade: Hard
Time: 6½ hrs
Distance: 14 km return
Ascent/descent: Total of 400 m over 2 peaks
Conditions: Sections of fire trail, duckboarding and steep rough rocky foot track, some rock hopping near summit; suitable for experienced walkers

More info: Wellington Park Management Trust T 6238 2176, Hobart City Council Infoline T 6278 0200

Getting there

Car: From the city drive up Davey St, keeping to the right to avoid a forced left turn down the Southern Outlet; keep straight as it becomes Huon Rad and follow signage to Mt Wellington; continue 4.9 km from The Springs and park in the small car park on the left

28 Collins Bonnet

Walk directions

1 The track is signed *Big Bend Trail* and starts at a white gateway. Initially it's a gravelled fire trail that leads along a wire fence on your right. The vegetation here is dominated by Yellow Gum (*Eucalyptus johnstonii*) which is endemic to mountain regions in southeastern Tasmania. The understorey contains a rich variety of hardy shrubs such as Daisy Bushes, Golden Rosemary, Dog Rose, Richeas and Heaths.

2 After a few minutes the track dips down steeply and Collins Cap, which lies north of Collins Bonnet, comes into view. The settlement down below on your right is Collinsvale. The bush here is alive

28 Collins Bonnet

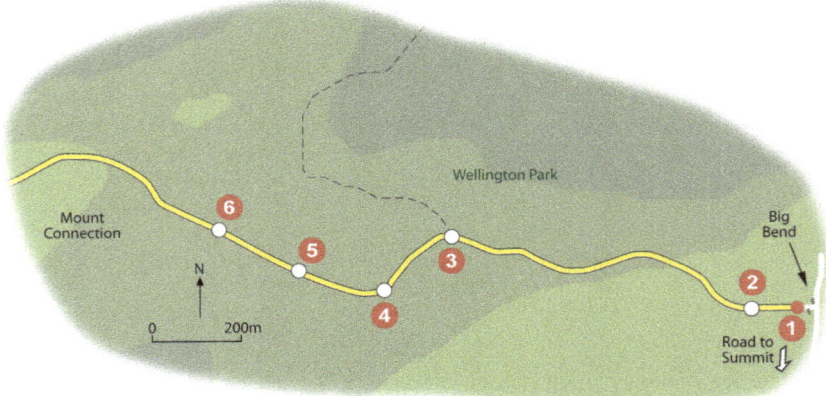

with birds and at different times you may hear both the Olive and Golden Whistler, Pardalotes and Honeyeaters. The gravel on the track is quite loose - watch your step. Pass a waterhole on your right and a *Track Closed* sign on your left, which also informs you that the Collins Bonnet Track turns off 250 metres along from here.

3 Turn left up a narrow, rocky foot track at the sign. This track is lined with masses of the attractive dainty Dog Rose (*Bauera rubioides*), with its small nodding flowers. You are passing Thark Ridge on your left and after a while you will reach a wooden sign on a yellow post to direct you to Collins Bonnet to the right.

4 After this right turn, Mt Direction comes into view and you will notice Pineapple Grass underfoot. Descend towards a swampy area: the source of Mountain River, which has cut a large valley to the southwest and flows into the Huon River near Huonville.

5 Cross the swamp via duckboarding. There's

Hobart environment – the Common Wombat (*Vombatus ursinus*)

As their scientific name suggests, these solidly built marsupials are 'bear-like' with their coarse dark brown fur and broad, clawed paws. Wombats are largely nocturnal but during winter can sometimes be spotted sunbaking or grazing during the day. They construct large burrows up to 20 metres long. Although their movements appear slow, they can develop surprisingly high speeds when startled. Their diet consists of native grasses, herbs, shrubs and roots and their preferred habitat is heathland. Womats give birth to one young joey which stays in the pouch for about six months and gains independence at about eighteen months of age.

28 Collins Bonnet

a change in the vegetation to patches of sedges, Coral Fern and Sphagnum Moss. The brick-shaped droppings you often see in prominent places atop rocks or logs along the track belong to the common wombat.

6 Head up through woodland on the far side of the swamp then begin to climb as you skirt around the northern top edge of Mt Connection. The track becomes rockier and there are small stretches of rock shelf and some boulder hopping as you near the top. Through the trees there are superb views down to Collinsvale and Mt Hull, its southeastern border. The prominent mountain slightly to the left, and nearer the

28 Collins Bonnet

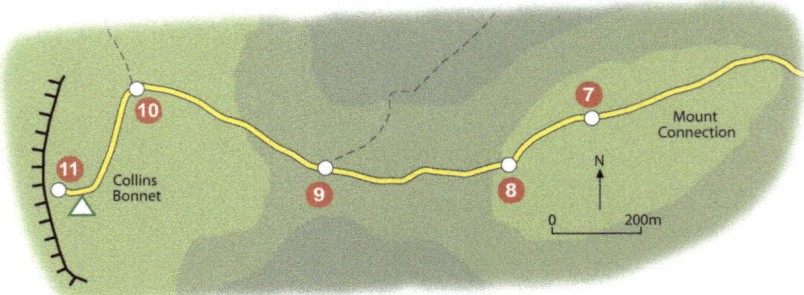

horizon, is Mt Dromedary. Further to your right you can clearly see where the Jordan River flows into the Derwent at Herdsmans Cove. The beautiful Tasmanian Waratah (see Walk 26) grows in rockier areas along the track and brightens up the bush during summer.

7 Shortly Collins Bonnet, your destination, comes into view as you reach an open, exposed area beside the track. On your right you can make out the Bowen Bridge crossing the Derwent River and the large building of the Derwent Entertainment Centre near it. The track passes a small rocky knoll on your right. You can climb it for a fine lookout from where, looking northwest can to see the FWD East West Trail which leads along the side of Collins Bonnet.

8 Return to the track and continue along it past another rocky outcrop. Some of the stunted eucalypts growing here are another Tasmanian endemic, the Snow Peppermint (*Eucalyptus coccifera*). As the track dips down steeply towards the saddle between Mt Connection and Collins Bonnet there are stunning views on your left into the Mountain River Valley and you can also see Franklin and make out Egg Island in the Huon River. The track finally emerges at a waterhole at the junction with the East West Trail.

9 Turn left and follow the East West Trail which you saw from the small lookout. After a short while the track begins to ascend steeply crossing numerous water run-offs. As you go higher you can look back and see the top of Mt Wellington with

Eyebright

Walk variation

You have the option to create a circuit by continuing along the East West Trail past the junction (see point 8) for about 3.3 kilometres until you reach the turn off to the *Big Bend Trail* on your right. Follow this to the Big Bend and the start point of your walk. This adds about 2.25 km to the total distance and leads along coarsely gravelled steep vehicular tracks.

28 Collins Bonnet

its large TV tower in the distance. Follow the East West Trail until you come to a sign - *Collins Bonnet Track* - with a large boulder near it.

10 Turn left here, along the steepening but well-trodden track that leads through a boggy section with more Pineapple Grass and is marked by the odd small rock cairn (and later with poles). Out of the bog, hop across the boulders which increase in size as you go up. At the trig point on the summit you are rewarded with magnificent views all around and stately dolerite boulders and columns.

11 On the summit you can enjoy a well-earned rest if the weather allows. The mountain west across the valley is Trestle Mountain. You may be lucky to see a Flame Robin flitting about and there are also many lizards to be found in this lofty environment. From the summit retrace your steps to the start point.

Bruny Island

The Aborigines called Bruny Island 'lunawannaalonna' and the name lives on in the small townships of Lunawanna and Alonnah. The island consists of two main land masses that are linked by a long narrow sand spit, the Neck. North Bruny is mainly low open grassland and forest, while South Bruny receives a higher rainfall, has spectacular dolerite sea cliffs, steep hills with pockets of rainforest, a large lagoon and secluded, sandy beaches. This variety of climate and landforms creates many different habitats and therefore a wonderfully diverse flora and fauna. As well as discovering some of the island's beaches, sea cliffs, heathlands and forests, you will also be able to spot many threatened and endemic species on this lovely 'island off an island' during the following walks.

The island is only 15 minutes away by ferry from Kettering on mainland Tasmania. Parks Passes apply to all walks described.

Mars Bluff

29 East Cloudy Head

If you enjoy expansive seascapes and rugged coastlines, you won't be disappointed during this lovely coastal walk. Bonuses are the flora, shaped by wind and seaspray, the high chance of encountering an echidna or two along the way and the view to the Cape Bruny Lighthouse.

At a glance

Grade: Medium
Time: 4½ hrs
Distance: Beach 6 km return *plus* track 7 km return
Ascent/descent: 300 m / 300 m
Conditions: Good hard beach section, disused 4WD track and narrow foot track for remainder; some short steep, rocky sections; exposed

More info: Parks and Wildlife Service, Adventure Bay, T 6293 1419

Getting there

Car: From the ferry terminal at Roberts Point follow signage to Alonnah and Lunawanna; turn left into Cloudy Bay Road and park at its end

29 East Cloudy Head

Walk directions

1 Go down to the beach and walk along it until after about three kilometres you see a 4WD track leading up into the bush on your left.

2 Continue your walk along this track, which crosses a small creek and passes a number of bush camp sites, a self registration box and a pit toilet. As you reach the far end and a turning circle, locate a small boulder on your right that marks the entrance to a narrow foot track.

3 Follow the foot track, leading down steeply, and keep left to reach a creek.

4 Turn left towards a walker's registration box then head over a small footbridge to cross the creek.

5 The track rises steeply up the creek bank and leads through an understorey of very tall Bracken Ferns. The bush here is regenerating well after fire and in spring and summer you will be able to see many different plants, including Flag Iris, Bluebells and Trigger Plants.

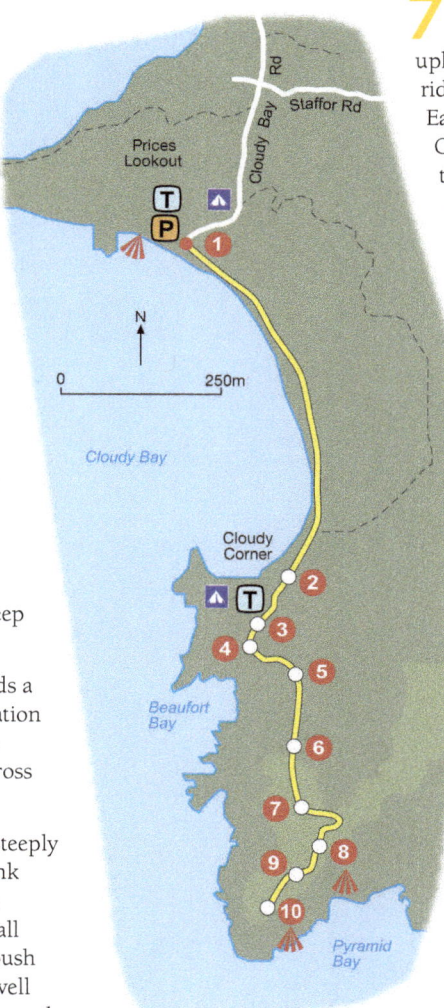

6 As you gain height, you will be able to see back to Cloudy Bay and ahead to Beaufort Point.

7 The track now curves left to lead uphill to the top of the ridge that leads onto East Cloudy Head. Once you've reached the ridge the climb becomes less steep, the track now curves right and you can see your destination, which consists of a smaller and a larger hill joined by a saddle, up ahead.

8 As the track leads slightly downhill to skirt the smaller hill along its northern side, pass through a small wooded area with stunted Stringy Bark trees.

Walk variation

Although the first part of this walk is a lovely solid walk along Cloudy Beach, where the tide and your vehicle permit, you can drive the full length of the beach and begin your walk at its southern end.

29 East Cloudy Head

Cloudy Corner campground

9 The track now rises steeply to make the final ascent, with truly spectacular views eastwards to the dolerite sea cliffs that line Pyramid Bay and the small group of islands known as The Friars to the south of Tasman Head (visible across the bay). The coastal heathland in this area displays a high diversity which includes both threatened and endemic heath species. You may encounter the odd echidna anywhere along the track. They are the only mammal that can be found during the day, with all others being nocturnal. You

Hobart environment – the Echidna *(Tachyglossus aculeatus)*

The Tasmanian echidna has more fur and less spines than the mainland forms and is also slightly larger, weighing up to four kilograms. It is an egg-laying mammal - a monotreme – and its closest living relative is the platypus, see walk 19. The eggs are soft shelled and the young hatch in about ten days and are suckled for three months before they are weaned. The echidna has poor eyesight and if you keep still when encountering one of these little fellows, you can observe them at very close range. They have been known to climb over the top of people's boots! They forage for ants, termites and other small invertebrates which they trap with their long sticky tongues.

29 East Cloudy Head

can often see where they have scratched around for ants, using their purpose-built, beak-like snout.

10 Keep left at a Y-junction near the summit (the track to the right is only short and leads to a lookout across the bay). Soon you will reach the trig and, just past it, a clear look out area. Here you are rewarded with panoramic views across Cloudy Bay and behind it the D'Entrecasteaux Channel and the Tasmanian mainland with Mt Wellington and the southern ranges clearly visible. Further to the southwest you may be able to spot the fish farms in Great Taylors Bay and Cape Bruny with its lighthouse. After you have enjoyed the views, and perhaps a picnic, retrace your steps to the start of the walk.

Summit of East Cloudy Head

29 East Cloudy Head

Out and about - Cape Bruny Lighthouse

The lighthouse was built during 1836-1838 after three major shipwrecks occurred in the area. It perches 103 metres above sea level and was built using convict labour to a design by John Lee Archer. It stands thirteen metres tall and operated for 150 years. To visit the lighthouse turn right at Lunawanna into the Lighthouse Road and drive to its end.

29 East Cloudy Head

View across Pyramid Bay to Tasman Head

30 Labillardiere Peninsula - Luggaboine

This eight by two kilometre-wide peninsula juts out into the D'Entrecasteaux Channel in a northwesterly direction. Two walks can be undertaken from the campground at the peninsula's southern end. You can opt to walk around the whole peninsular (a five hour circuit which begins along a disused 4WD track through coastal vegetation and includes a climb over 142 metre-high Mt Bleak, a walk along Butlers Beach at the northern end and a return through rocky bushland along Great Taylors Bay), or you can choose the shortened version described below where you turn inland at less than a quarter of the distance to cut across the peninsula and rejoin the Labillardiere Peninsula track at the edge of Great Taylors Bay. Both walks begin at the same start point. The peninsula consists mainly of dolerite with a cover of windblown sand. It is aptly named for La Billardiere, the French botanist: its heathlands contain many botanical delights for most of the year.

At a glance

Grade: Easy
Time: 1½ hrs
Distance: 5 km circuit
Ascent/descent: 60 m / 60 m
Conditions: Well formed track with some shade
More info: Parks and Wildlife Service, Adventure Ba,y T6293 1419

Getting there

Car: From the ferry terminal at Roberts Point follow signs to Alonnah and Lunawanna; turn right into Lighthouse Rd, right again into Old Jetty Rd and park in the visitor car park to the left just after entering the Jetty Beach camp ground

30 Labillardiere Peninsula - Luggaboine

Walk directions

1 The start of the narrow track has a sign and a walker registration box and initially leads through a marshy area with with Melaleucas and She-oaks.

2 The track rises gently uphill into bushland. During December there is a stunning profusion of Flag Iris and the spectacular red Christmas Bells, which grow beneath the stunted eucalypts.

3 Turn right at a T-junction with a disused vehicular track to continue your walk. Shortly you will gain views across Standaway Bay.

4 After a short while the track dips down toward the coast and after about 45 minutes you will reach a signposted track junction.

5 Turn right into a wider, mown firebreak - the shortcut track across the peninsula. It leads through low coastal vegetation and a wetland on your right, which allows you to see the views ahead towards the Tasmanian mainland with Mt Wellington a prominent landmark on the horizon.

6 The shortcut track descends into woodland with She-oaks, Banksia and Hakea and an understorey of Bracken and Christmas Bells. The track leads along a small watercourse emerging at a swamp.

7 Another five minutes and you are at the junction with the Peninsula track. Turn right, following signage to Jetty Beach. You will cross the watercourse and go up its bank then gradually downhill until you emerge at a small beach. Walk along the beach to its far end and continue on the track.

8 The final section leads inland, crossing three minor watercourses via wooden walkways, through bushland until you reach the lower end of the Jetty Beach camp ground. Walk through the campground to the start point.

30 Labillardiere Peninsula - Luggaboine

Hobart history - Tasmania's *French Connection*

In 1791 the French government sent an expedition of two frigates to Tasmanian waters with the objectives of making scientific discoveries and surveys and, secondly, searching for Jean-Francois de **La Perouse**, who had gone missing with his two ships three years earlier after leaving Botany Bay. The expedition, led by Antoine Raymond Joseph de **Bruni d'Entrecasteaux** on the 500 ton *La Recherche* and the similarly sized ship *L'Esperance*, under the command of Jean-Michel **Huon de Kermandec**, reached Tasmania (then called Van Diemen's Land) in 1792 and anchored in the vicinity of Bruny Island for about five weeks. During this time they charted the area and named many features. You can find the bolded names on most maps of Tasmania.

Flora and fauna with French Names

Jaques-Julien Houton de La Billardiere was the accompanying botanist of the expedition who collected not only plants but also animals, including fish and birds. He also produced detailed accounts of the Aboriginal people and their way of life. The beautiful *Billardiera longiflora* (Mountain Blue Berry), *Poa labillardiera* (Silver Tussock), the *Ctenotus labillardieri* (Red Legged Skink) and the *Thylogale billardierii* (Tasmanian Pademelon) all bear his name.

30 Labillardiere Peninsula - Luggaboine

Out and about - Landscape features with French Names

One harbour received the name Recherche Bay, the channel between the Tasmanian mainland and the island to the east was named D'Entrecasteaux Channel, the island became Bruny Island and a mountain in the distance was called Mt La Perouse. Some of the other landscape features that were named by this expedition were the Huon River, the Kermandie River (which flows into the Huon at Geeveston), Port Esperance and Esperance Point (west of Bruny across the Channel), Mt Bruny on Bruny Island and Bruny Island's westernmost tip, the Labillardiere Peninsula.

31 Cape Queen Elizabeth

This walk to the northern end of Adventure Bay is within the Bruny Island Neck Game Reserve and offers a wonderful variety of features ranging from open, dry sclerophyll bushland (the preferred home of Bennetts wallabies), a lagoon, beaches and large dunes, a quaint little hut, a shearwater rookery and finally - to top it all off - fantastic views from the summit of the Cape. It is a good idea to check tides before setting off, as at low tide you can walk around the base of Mars Bluff which juts into the sea between Neck Beach and Miles Beach, whereas at high tide you need to use the track over the top of Mars Bluff, which takes a little longer.

At a glance

Grade: Medium
Time: Along beach 3 hrs return, via top of Mars Bluff 3 ½ hrs
Distance: 12 km return via Mars Bluff
Ascent/descent: 80 m / 80 m
Conditions: Initially a 4WD track, then well trodden foot track. No track markers, but signs or marker at major track junctions. Slightly confusing network of tracks around the summit. Some shady areas, dunes and beaches.
More info: Parks and Wildlife Service, Adventure Bay T62931419
Tidal Information
Ferry timetable T62736725

Getting there

Car: From the ferry terminal at Roberts Point follow signs to Adventure Bay. Just before the airstrip turn left into a small car park at the start of the walk.

31 Cape Queen Elizabeth

Walk directions

1 Enter the old vehicular track by walking around the boom gate across the track and follow it as it heads off in a straight line along the edge of the forest with a farm fence on your left. You'll pass a walk registration box as you continue along the track. The dry sclerophyll forest of various Eucalypts contains Wattles, Banksias, Teatrees with Tasmanian flax lily and sedges as groundcover.

2 After about five minutes, and an old gateway, the track begins to curve to the left to continue in a southeasterly direction, becoming sandier. There are some beautiful specimens of the Native Cherry (*Exocarpus cupressiformis*) here.

3 In about a quarter of an hour Cape Queen Elizabeth becomes visible up ahead and the vegetation turns into coastal heath. The taller shrubs are Teatree, Swamp Heath and Boobialla. As you pass Big Lagoon on your right, you can observe a number of lagoon and estuary birds such as plovers, ducks and herons. Continue along the track, which narrows here and cuts through tall Bracken Ferns passing Little Lagoon on your left. Overhead you

can often hear pardalotes, wrens and honeyeaters.

4 The track continues through a small woodland as it passes the lagoons, then rises to cross four dunes before you are presented with great ocean views. Note how the sand changes colour from white to yellow along the way. Looking back you can see the lagoons in the foreground, and all along Adventure Bay, with the Fluted Cape at its far end.

5 After a short time the track goes left to run parallel to the beach. It then dips down to reach a brown sign giving you the option to take the beach route to Moorina Bay and Miles Beach at low tide or to climb Mars Bluff to reach Miles Beach.

163

31 Cape Queen Elizabeth

Mars Bluff

6 Choose wisely, but even at high tide it is well worth the effort to walk down to the base of the bluff to inspect the sea and weather carved mud and siltstone rock formations and sea caves there.

7 The track over the top of Mars Bluff rises steeply through She-oaks and sedges to reach a Y-junction in about ten minutes.

8 Keep to the right and cross a small clearing with a *Walking Track* sign at the other end. The track sidles along the contour of the Bluff with a very steep drop down to the beach on your right. Pass through another woodland with a canopy of stunted Eucalyptus obliqua, then go downhill through taller coastal shrubs and down some wooden steps that lead onto the top of a massive dune.

9 Make your way down to the beach and walk along it until you see Miles creek come in from your left. Here you can make a small detour by walking along the eastern side of the creek where you

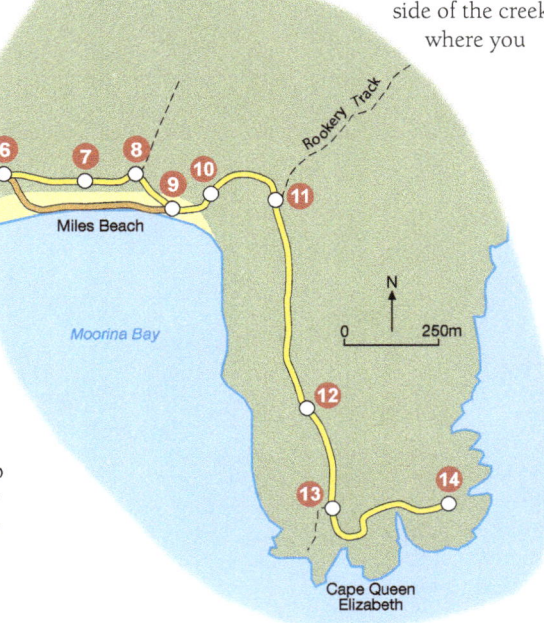

31 Cape Queen Elizabeth

will find an interesting small hut perched on top of the bank.

10 Return to the beach and locate the tall, rough stick with a yellow plastic bag tied to it that marks the continuation of the track. This rises steeply up the dune and turns into a vehicular track at a *Walking Track* sign. A little further along you will come across the junction with the Rookery track that comes in from the left.

11 Turn right and head south, skirting along the contour of Cape Queen Elizabeth and passing through some beautiful forest with Blue Gums and Blackwoods. The track becomes less distinct and soon goes through shorter

Base of Mars Bluff

31 Cape Queen Elizabeth

vegetation, then crosses a small gully and later a shearwater rookery covered in a bright green succulent plant.

12 After another stretch of forest the terrain opens up to great views across Adventure Bay and beyond.

13 Take a left turn for the last, short steep ascent to the top of the Cape, where you will find a small rock cairn marking the spot. Time to enjoy the panorama and perhaps a rest and a snack.

14 This area is criss-crossed with tracks so take care to pick your way back down towards the main track, then turn right and retrace your steps back to your starting point.

Boobialla

Hobart environment - Little Penguin (*Eudyptula minor novaehollandiae*)

These little fellows are the smallest in the Penguin family, only 32 to 34 cm short and weighing about 1.2 kg. They are only found in Australia and New Zealand with a distribution that ranges from Fremantle in Western Australia to Sydney and includes Tasmania. Their favourite habitat is rocky shorelines in close proximity to fishing grounds. They feed at sea during the day and return to their nesting colonies after dark to rest. They call to each other before coming ashore in small groups and interact with others in a very sociable manner before retiring to their own burrow. Their nesting season is from September to February.

31 Cape Queen Elizabeth

view to east from the summit

Hobart environment - The Neck

Consisting of a 100-metre wide strip of towering dunes, this is Tasmania's longest isthmus and links North and South Bruny. A set of wooden stairs leads up to the Truganini lookout from where you can see this impressive landform, shaped as sea levels rose at the end of the last ice age. It is now a wildlife sanctuary and contains little penguin and muttonbird rookeries that can be seen from the stairway of the observation deck.

32 Fluted Cape

While Cape Queen Elizabeth sits at the northern end of Adventure Bay, Fluted Cape - with its 272 metres high dolerite sea cliffs with Grass Point at their base - shapes the southern end. This walk passes through tall forest dominated by Tasmanian Blue Gums to reach Grass Point. As you climb the cape you will see its beautiful organ pipe formation, pass a few natural sculptures along the way and stare in awe at the boiling sea far below. A wonderful walk, but not suitable for very young children.

At a glance

Grade: Medium/hard
Time: 2.5 hrs
Distance: 5.4 km circuit
Ascent/descent: 270 m / 270 m
Conditions: Mostly level to Grassy Point; steep climb to the top of the cape, passing close to the unfenced cliff edge, descent through open bushland.
More info: Parks and Wildlife Service, Adventure Bay T 6293 1419

Getting there

Car: From the ferry terminal at Roberts Point follow signs to Adventure Bay; drive through Adventure Bay and Cookville to a designated car park just past the small bay that Adventure Bay Cruises operate from

Grass Point

32 Fluted Cape

Walk directions

1 The start of the walking track is just past the boat ramp. Go down to the beach at the *Fluted Cape Walk* sign and an interpretive sign about the history of the bay. Turn right and walk to the end of the beach, then right again near the bank at the far end. Walk between the creek and bank until you see the entrance to the track, which leads up the bank to join a wide gravel path.

2 Turn left, and follow the shoreline beneath tall Blue Gums and She-oaks and through an understorey of saggs. This

East Cove Beach

32 Fluted Cape

type of forest is home to the threatened Swift Parrot.

3 Keep left at a Y-junction, and after about five minutes you will pass a small pond and a *South Bruny National Park* entry sign. This is the start and end point of the Fluted Cape circuit. Take the clockwise option by keeping left.

4 The track narrows and becomes rocky, heading through Blackwoods, She-oaks and Native Cherries. In a while there is some interpretive signage informing you about the history of the whaling industry in Adventure Bay.

5 The northern most point - the open 'wallaby lawn' area of Grass Point – is reached in less than half an hour. If you are lucky you may be able to spot a Tasmanian Pademelon in this area, particularly towards the end of the day.

6 Continue along the track, marked with a brown sign, which heads steeply uphill to the right. There are many birds in the trees above, including rosellas, wattlebirds, whistlers, thornbills and wrens. Keep right at a Y-junction after about five minutes and, shortly after, you'll get your first glimpses of the Fluted Cape up ahead.

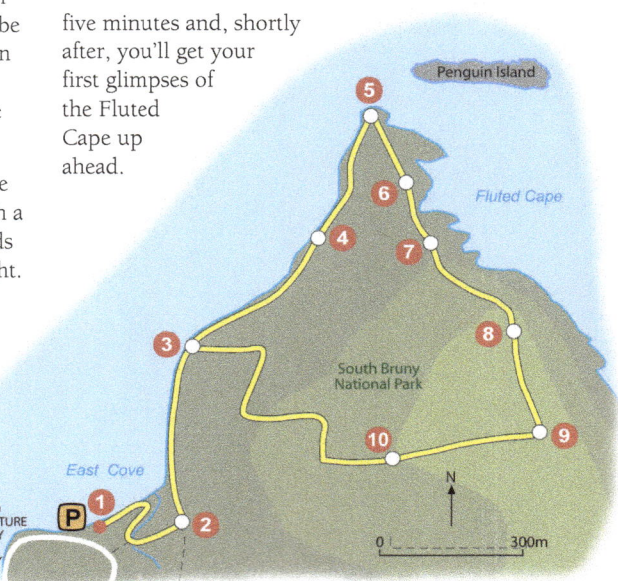

170

32 Fluted Cape

Note how the cliffs on your left are rapidly increasing in height.

7 At the first major level area on the climb there's a natural sculpture, reminiscent of the Easter Island statues.

8 The track dips down into a saddle before again rising steeply, passing some more rock features and heading closely along the cliff top. A brown sign tells you that you have climbed 272 metres and are at the top of the rise – it therefore also marks the beginning of the downhill part of your walk.

9 After having enjoyed the lofty height take the downhill track which leads in a westerly direction through beautiful dry sclerophyll forest with Stringy Bark and Blue Gums and a species-rich

Hobart environment - Native Cherry (*Exocarpus cupressiformis*)

This attractive small tree is somewhat of an oddity in several ways. It can grow to a height of eight metres and looks a bit like a Cyprus (*'cupressi' 'formis'* - formed like a Cyprus), but actually has leaves that have been reduced to very small scales while the stems have taken over the function of photosynthesis. *'Exo'* (outer) and *'carpus'* (seed) indicates that the seed is found on the outside of the fruit. The four to six millimeter long fruit is globular and sits on a short stalk. As it ripens the stalk swells and turns red, like an inside out cherry. This part is edible, but the green 'nut' on its end needs to be discarded. It is thought that Native Cherries are parasitic on the roots of other plants around them and this is why they are hard to propagate - you never see them sold in nurseries.

32 Fluted Cape

understorey that contains Guitar Plants, Tasmanian Flax Lily, Olearia, Banksia and Native Cherries. The descent is not as steep, as the track zig-zags as you near the coast to maintain a fairly even gradient.

10 The track passes through a larger stand of Native Cherries, sheltering some fine specimens, before reaching the end of the loop at the junction with the wider track you came up on. Turn left and walk back to the starting point.

Hobart environment - Tasmanian Pademelon or Rufous Wallaby (*Thylogale billardierii*)

These wallabies are now endemic to Tasmania, although they could once be found on the Australian mainland. They are abundant and prefer to graze at night in clearings next to dense forest areas where they hide during the day. Pademelons are short (about one metre) and stocky (females average about four kilograms in weight) with short legs and a short tail. They have a very thick, dark brown to grey coat to keep them warm during Tasmania's cool winters. Their diet consists of short grasses, herbs and mosses. Most of the joeys are born in early winter and live in the mother's pouch for over six months, becoming independent after seven to eight months.

32 Fluted Cape

Fluted Cape

Hobart history – Bruny Island
Abel Tasman was the first to sight Bruny Island but did not land. Cook, Furneaux, D'Entrecasteaux, Flinders and Bligh all landed at Adventure Bay at different times. From 1820 to 1850 Bruny was part of the whaling industry and supported a permanent whaling station with 80 residents. Whale oil was used for cooking and lighting. You can visit the Bligh Museum at Adventure Bay for in depth information on Bruny Island's European history.

Further afield

If you follow the River Derwent northwards to Granton, then westwards to New Norfolk and onto Westerway and Mt Field National Park you will be taking a trip through a significant part of Tasmania's colonial history. You will be passing through one of Australia's oldest towns, with Australia's oldest mental hospital, and remnants of the once thriving hop industry which was established in 1804. From the quaint village of Westerway you will follow the Tyenna River (a tributary of the Derwent) upstream to Mt Field National Park, Tasmania's first reserve and oldest national park. The walks in this chapter will acquaint you with some of the main features along this historic journey.

St Lukes, Richmond

33 New Norfolk

New Norfolk, named for the group of Norfolk Islanders who settled here in 1808 and one of Australia's oldest towns, straddles the Derwent River about 36 kilometres northwest of Hobart. Local produce was shipped along the River Derwent to Hobart and hops became a major industry, with picturesque oast houses (hop drying kilns) still dotting the countryside. Hopfields were traditionally sheltered by rows of tall poplars and remnants of these hedges can also still be found throughout the Derwent Valley. They and a number of other deciduous trees make a colourful display in autumn. This walk leads along the Derwent, through the town and past the historic Willow Court asylum site, returning to the start via the Lachlan River, a tributary to the Derwent.

At a glance

Grade: Easy
Time: 2 hrs
Distance: 5.9 km circuit
Conditions: An unfenced cliff top, some steep steps and a highway crossing; dogs ok on a leash
More info: Derwent Valley Access Centre, www.tco.asn.au

Getting there

Car: From Hobart use the Brooker and Lyell Highways to reach New Norfolk; look for a large sign to *Tynwald Park* and turn (right) into it; follow this along the right-hand side of various picnic areas and playing fields to its end

Bus: O'Driscoll Coaches, T 6249 8880, www.derwentvalleylink.com.au

33 New Norfolk

Walk directions

1 A wide gravelled track leads off to the left (west) from the car park and over a small footbridge across the Lachlan River, which flows into the Derwent River near here. Follow the track past some ponds (for sewerage treatment) that are fringed by cumbungi and reeds and are a haven for waterfowl. It soon curves to the left to wind along the Derwent. Across the river you will see imposing siltstone cliffs, dating back some 250 million-odd years to the Permian Period, towering over the river's edge with only just enough room to accommodate the Boyer Road and a disused railway line.

2 After a short distance the track swings left away from the river and up a small rise to continue along a wire fence on the left, crossing beneath some transmission lines. Soon you reach the top of some siltstone cliffs on your right, from which there are views up and down the river (take care though, particularly with children, as the cliff top is not fenced!). Continue until you see the sign *Walking Tack via Esplanade*.

3 Turn right to descend, on a narrow, steep track through some large boulders with concrete steps and a steel handrail, back to the riverbank. The track emerges onto a couple of small grassy areas and the Esplanade, where there's a viewing area over the river.

4 Continue along the riverbank, passing a caravan park and sports ground on your left and a boat ramp on your right, and cross the end of Ferry Street. The playing fields now on your left are the venue for the Derwent Valley Autumn Festival,

33 New Norfolk

held annually in April. There are picnic tables and seats all along the Esplanade, shaded by mature exotic, deciduous trees such as Oaks, Elms and Maples. Many ducks are waiting for a crumb to fall their way here! There's a kiosk about halfway along the esplanade, open from 0900 to 1600 in summer and 1000 to 1500 in winter, which has dinghies and fishing rods for hire. Heading further along, after passing a fishing platform (from which trout can reliably be caught), a picnic shelter and BBQ area mark the far end of the Esplanade.

5 Walk past the car barrier at the end of the Esplanade and continue a short way along the river, past a huge conifer and other exotic trees, to an old bridge abutment. After viewing 'Woodbridge', a gentleman's residence built in 1825, turn back and leave the Esplanade via a sealed path with a steel handrail that leads into Bridge Street. Turn left into Montagu Street and walk along it until you reach the Bush Inn, Australia's oldest continuously licensed hotel. Carefully cross Montagu Street (which is the Lyell Highway) and walk straight ahead uphill along Burnett Street. On the right there's a small white church, St Pauls Uniting Church, built in 1836 and claimed to be the oldest church still in use in Australia.

6 When you reach High Street make a small side trip by turning left to the end of the street, then walk through the gardens of Arthur Square to view St Matthews Anglican Church, slightly to your right at the far end of the gardens. This is Australia's second oldest church!

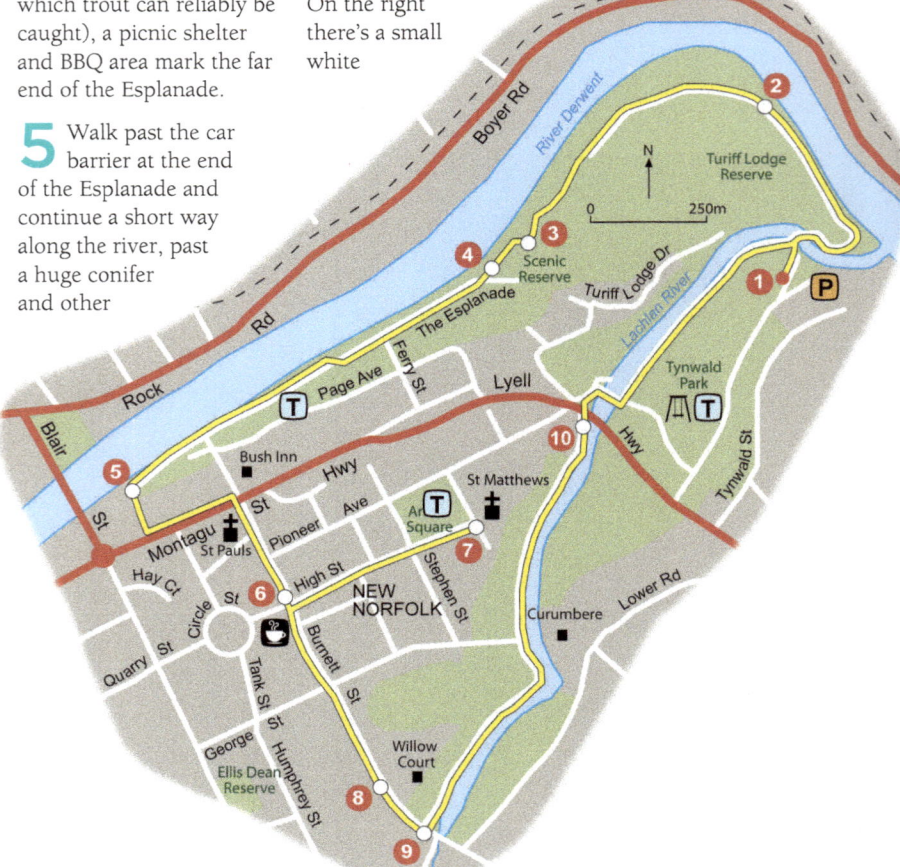

178

33 New Norfolk

Woodbridge

St Matthews

Nurses Home

8 After inspecting some of the buildings of this historic mental asylum, walk down 'The Avenue' (Millbrook Road) towards the Lachlan River and locate the track off to the left, just before the bridge, that heads north along the riverbank.

9 Follow the river downstream, skirting the town centre to your left. Across the river, to the right, you will see a large building with oast house replicas incorporated into its architectural design. This is 'Corumbene', a nursing home for the aged.

10 The riverside track eventually passes under the Lyell Highway and, soon afterwards, crosses the river via a small footbridge to the right, leading onto the western edge of Tynwald Park. Turn left and walk along by the playing fields until you find your starting point.

7 Return to Burnett Street and turn left, heading along Burnett Street and crossing George Street to reach the old entrance gate to Willow Court Asylum complex. Rumour has it that an eight foot tall brick barrel drain, with the profile of a 50 cent coin, runs under this street all the way from the Bush Inn to Willow Court, but as it's under a foot of concrete no one can find entrances to it!

33 New Norfolk

Hobart history - Willow Court

The 18-hectare precinct of Willow Court, formerly known as the Royal Derwent Psychiatric Hospital, was until its closure Australia's oldest mental hospital on its original site and has now been heritage listed. It was built in 1830-31 as a military hospital and later grew into the largest colonial hospital and mental asylum in the southern hemisphere. Architectural influences from early colonial days up to the 1960s are represented in the buildings. Of course there are a lot of ghost stories about this eerie site. The hospital was closed in the late 90s and the site was acquired by the local council with a view to develop it into a tourist attraction to rival Port Arthur. To date parts of the site have been re-developed into tourist accommodation, luxury retirement units, a restaurant and a museum.

Asylum wall

Hobart history - the hop industry

Hops were first brought into Tasmania in 1804; the brewing of beer was seen as a healthier and cheaper alternative to spirits and was therefore encouraged by government. The first crop of hops was harvested in 1818 by William Shoobridge and the Shoobridge family farmed properties at Bushy Park, just north of New Norfolk, for the next seven decades, 65 years of which centred around continuous hop production. It became the most successful hop growing area in the southern hemisphere.

33 New Norfolk

Derwent Valley

34 Lake Dobson and Pandani Grove

Here's an easy wander along a lake shore, where many of Tasmania's sub-alpine plants such as Mountain Berries, Waratah and Snow Gum can be found. If you are lucky enough to be able to visit after a snowfall, this area becomes a winter wonderland where the world's tallest heath, Pandani (*Richea pandanifolia*) dominates the scenery. These upright plants are picturesque at any time of the year and are reminiscent of family groups with their variation in size. Adults can reach a height of nine metres.

At a glance

Grade: Easy
Time: 50 mins
Distance: 2.2 km return
Ascent/Descent: 40 m / 40 m
Conditions: Well formed gravel track with boarded and rocky sections, mostly shady and sheltered, suitable for families; park entry fees apply

More info: Parks and Wildlife Service, www.parks.tas.gov.au

Getting there

Car: Mt Field NP is 75 km northwest of Hobart on the Maydena Rd; drive past the park visitor centre, turn left and continue for about 16 km to the Lake Dobson car park

Pencil Pine

34 Lake Dobson and Pandani Grove

Walk directions

1 The track begins at a large blue sign - *Ski Fields, Alpine Tracks* - and heads along a fence down to a boardwalk with a wooden, lakeside viewing platform on the right. Here, you can see into the beautifully clear waters of this glacial lake, and perhaps see an Anaspides, a freshwater shrimp that is described as a living fossil because very similar crustaceans have been found as fossils in European and North American rocks dating back some 250 million years.

2 Turn left and walk along the lake's shore. The very prickly foliage is the endemic *Richea scoparia* plant, locally known as just 'Scoparia', a smaller cousin to the Pandani. Bushwalkers try to avoid walking through it, as it has a habit of penetrating waterproof clothing with its sharp pointy, leaves. However, when in flower, this plant is a delight with its candle like flower spikes that range in colour from cream to pink, orange and red.

3 After a few minutes the Wellington Ski Club Hut appears on your left. Continue along the boardwalk by the lakeside, passing patches of alpine moorland species growing under the canopy of Snow Gums and Pencil Pines. In a couple more minutes, after crossing a stream via a small wooden bridge, a number of the distinctive Pandani plants will appear in view.

4 Pass a track leading off to the left, which leads to the *Skifields and alpine tracks* (the track you will return on), and continue on the *Lake Circuit via Pandani Grove* track that follows the lake shore. The lichen covered dolerite boulders along the way increase in size and are a decorative feature in their own right. After crossing a few more minor streams you will reach the northern end of the lake and will be able to spot the Hobart Walking Club Hut across the water.

5 Also at this point you will enter Pandani Grove with a large numbers of picturesque Pandani plants standing in mixed age and size groups. The track continues in a northeasterly direction through this delightful grove, then heads

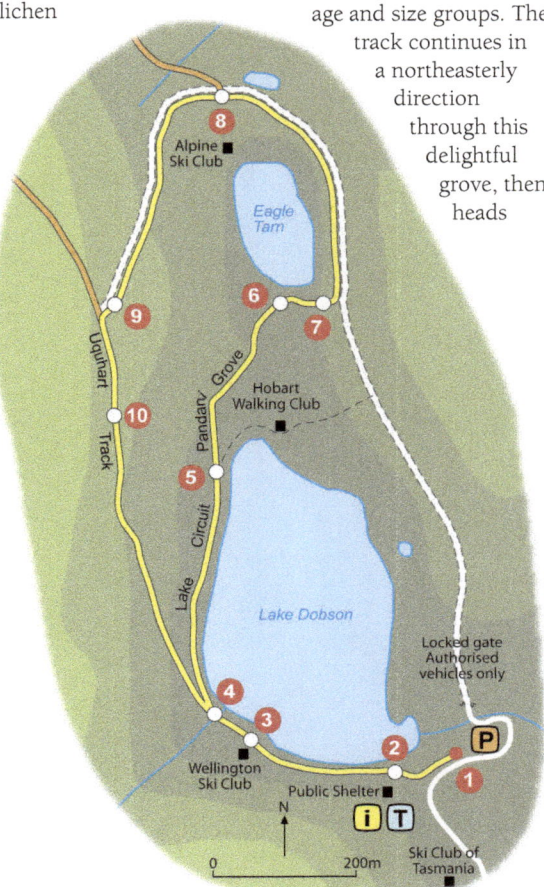

183

34 Lake Dobson and Pandani Grove

Snow Gums

through a small wet forest of Snow Gums, Myrtle and Pencil Pines.

6 Shortly after crossing a stream, Eagle Tarn, which lies to the north of Lake Dobson, comes into view on your left. You can see the hut of the Alpine Ski Club across the Tea Tree edged tarn. In summer native water lilies line the tarn and you will be able to hear a veritable frog's concert.

7 A short distance further, the track joins a vehicular track which, if you turn right, leads back to the Lake Dobson car

Eagle Tarn

Out and about - Russell Falls

A ten-minute stroll along a level foot track will take you from the Mt Field Visitor Centre to the much photographed falls that expose old mudstones laid down during the Permian ages. It is their beauty that first prompted the survey of 300 surrounding acres so that the area could be made into Tasmania's first reserve, in 1885. Mt Field also became Tasmania's first National Park when it was finally proclaimed such in 1916.

34 Lake Dobson and Pandani Grove

park. However, for a more interesting loop, turn left to follow the gravel road as it heads around the eastern and northern banks of Eagle Tarn. As you gain height Mawson Plateau becomes occasionally visible across the tarn on your left.

8 Pass the turn-off to *Platypus Tarn, Lake Seal, Lake Webster and Twilight Tarn* and a wide gravel area and ignore a rough track on your right, as the vehicular track curves left to go along the top contour of Eagle Tarn. The track rises more steeply to gain about twenty metres in height until you reach a sharp right hand bend in the road.

9 Go straight ahead here to enter the Urquhart foot track. You will descend gradually at first as you enjoy the view into the glacial valley in which Lake Dobson and Eagle Tarn are nestled. The colourful trunks of the *Alpine Yellow Gum (Eucalyptus subcrenulata)* can look particularly attractive in moist conditions in this area.

10 After crossing another stream the track descends more steeply towards the shore of Lake Dobson and joins the lakeside track which leads back to your start point.

Pandani

Hobart environment - Pandani (*Richea pandanifolia*)

The plant genus Richea is named for the French botanist C. A. Riche who travelled with Bruni D'Entrcasteaux (see Walk 30). Of the eleven Richea species, nine are Tasmanian endemics, including the Pandani. These tall heath plants are found in wet mountain forests in the southwest of Tasmania. They are generally unbranched and their persistent dead leaves form grassy 'skirts' around their bases. The tops of their trunks bear leaves three to four centimetre wide and more than a metre long, reminiscent of pineapple plants. The leaves taper to a point that often ends in a curl. Red or pink flowers are borne in the leaf axils.

35 Tarn Shelf

Many Tasmanian bushwalkers are familiar with the much-loved Tarn Shelf, which becomes a Mecca in autumn for the deciduous, endemic small tree affectionately known as 'fagus'. Small lakes and tarns on the Tarn Shelf are edged with this plant and its colourful displays are well worth the effort of this walk. At other times of the year you can enjoy the alpine plant communities found here which include pineapple grass and snow gums. You can also look for tiny shrimp in the tarns, watch Wedge Tailed Eagles and hear the musical call of the Black Currawong. The distinctive mountain scenery is dominated by Jurassic dolerite, with its columnar structure, and glacial features such as Lake Seal.

At a glance

Grade: Hard
Time: 5½ hrs
Distance: 14 km circuit
Ascent/Descent: 250 m / 250 m
Conditions: Steep descents and ascents, rocky with intermittent duck boarding; creek crossings, do not attempt in poor weather; best time summer and autumn; park entry fees apply

More info: Parks and Wildlife Service, www.parks.tas.gov.au; EPIRBs can be hired at Service Tasmania, Hobart T 1300 135513

Getting there

Car: Mt Field NP is 75 km northwest of Hobart on the Maydena Rd; drive past the park visitor centre, turn left and continue for about 16 km to the Lake Dobson car park

35 Tarn Shelf

Walk directions

1 Begin your walk by going to the bottom of the car park and locating a barred vehicle access road on your left. Walk along this for about 750 metres, leaving Lake Dobson to your left, until you reach a brown sign to *Platypus Tarn, Lake Seal, Lake Webster and Twilight Tarn* on your right.

2 Turn into this narrow, rocky foot track which heads in a northerly direction, descending fairly steeply - it can be quite wet at times. Pass a track to the left leading off to Platypus Tarn and continue downhill. Further along you can enjoy views, to your left, across to Mt Bridges, which sits

35 Tarn Shelf

above Platypus Tarn, and Lake Seal. In autumn the colourful berries of the Epacrid plant family are present in the understorey. Further downhill there are small tarns fringed with pineapple grass.

3 Pass the Y-junction with the track leading off to Lake Seal and keep right toward Lake Webster. Soon you will find the much photographed Fairy Tarn on your left. Continue on the track northwards until Lake Webster becomes visible. The track leads through Cutting Grass and Button Grass and begins to curve to the left to skirt around the northern side of the lake.

4 The track southeast to Lake Fenton branches off from here. Ignore it and follow the *Twilight Tarn – 45 min* sign, soon crossing the outflow of the lake on a steel foot bridge. The track then rises steeply in a westerly direction towards Twilight Tarn and the northern end of Tarn Shelf. In autumn many species of fungi can be found here. A couple of near-level sections during this climb allow you to catch your breath. Shortly Twilight Tarn will come into view and you will reach a junction. The track straight ahead leads, in about 100 metres, to a hut at the northern end of Twilight Tarn - a welcoming two-roomed shelter for a meal break. In one of the rooms you can find a small display of some

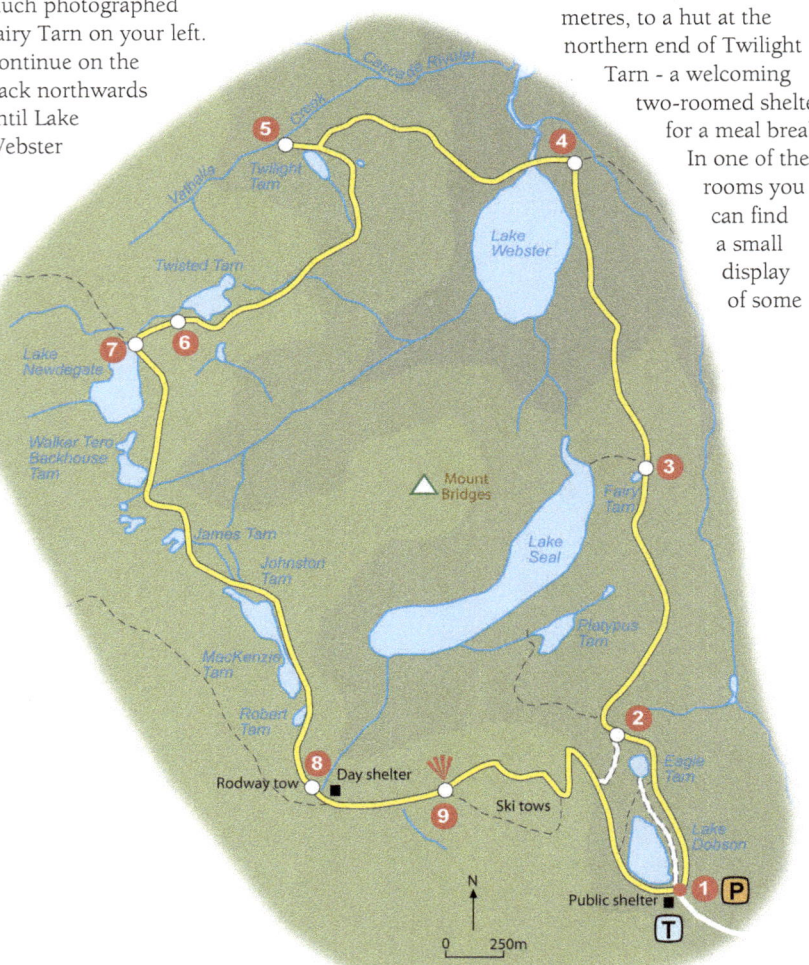

35 Tarn Shelf

interesting bushwalking memorabilia.

5 Return to the junction and turn right to continue in a southeasterly direction along Twilight Tarn, climbing gradually. As you gain height snow markers appear along the track. The wide creek that feeds the tarn is on your right; you'll cross it near its source towards the top of the shelf. Then turn southwest and climb a small distance up through a boulder field and past a number of small tarns to arrive at the watershed, with Twisted Tarn visible below. The conifer skeletons in this area are old Pencil Pines that were destroyed in a fire and have not regenerated.

6 The track descends southwest, leaving

Twisted Tarn to your right. Soon, some wooden steps lead onto a duck boarded T-junction. The track to the right leads to Newdegate Hut, at the northern end of Lake Newdegate, another popular resting spot.

7 From the T-junction continue south along Lake Newdegate over the top of a hill and back down again towards Backhouse Tarn, crossing the top of the creek that feeds Lake Webster below. The track along the Tarn Shelf has been loved to death and braided by thousands of visitors over the years; the Tasmanian Parks and Wildlife Service is currently undertaking work to rehabilitate it and define it into a single hardened track

35 Tarn Shelf

to better accommodate the traffic. Keep heading along in a southeasterly direction until you reach a ski tow and the Rodway Day Shelter hut. Most importantly, enjoy the beauty and tranquillity of this special place as you make your way.

8 After a well earned rest in the Rodway hut, climb up the steep embankment towards a large aluminium sign and a T-junction. Turn left (east) and follow the duckboard track. Looking down into the deep valley to your left you will see Lake Seal, a prominent glacial feature.

9 When you reach a crossroads, do not turn left or right but continue on to the east. The duckboarding ends and the track descends steeply through a rocky area and a fine stand of Snow Gums, past a final lookout to Lake Seal to emerge at some ski huts and a gravel access road. Follow the road downhill to its second major left-hand bend and turn right into the narrow, signposted *Urquhart Track* that soon joins the *Pandani Grove Track* along the foreshore of Lake Dobson and finally heads back around to the car park.

Hobart environment – glacial features

The Lake Seal Valley is a cirque which was gouged out by a glacier during a, geologically speaking, recent ice age. The gouged out boulders became stuck in the glacier as it crept down the valley and when it melted the rocks were dropped to leave behind a dam-like structure known as a moraine. This is nature's way of creating a tarn or lake - no bulldozers needed!

35 Tarn Shelf

Hobart environment - 'Fagus'

This deciduous beech, with the botanical name *Nothofagus gunnii,* is the only Tasmanian native plant that looses it's leaves in autumn. The leaves are roundish, small and crinkly, with scalloped edges, making them quite distinctive even when they are green. The plant grows to a height of 1.5 to 5 metres, depending on the harshness of the environment, and is a cousin to the much taller *Nothofagus cunninghamii* or Myrtle Beech, a rainforest tree that can reach a height of 50 metres. Myrtle is prized by furniture makers and woodworkers for its beautiful reddish-pink timber.

36 Lake Nicholls

If you prefer the tranquillity of bushland and birdsong and don't mind a rocky track, this lesser known short walk, part of the longer Mt Field East Circuit, is for you. It is particularly enjoyable in autumn when there are many different fungi to be found along the way and when the stunning red flowering Climbing Heath (*Prionotes cerinthoides*) can be spotted adorning tree trunks or as a ground cover. A number of mountain berries, snow berries, native currants and native pepperberries in a range of colours grow in the understorey, adding interest, and a well kept hut by the lakeside makes a great destination for a picnic. Older children usually enjoy this track for its rockiness.

At a glance

Grade: Medium
Time: 1¾ hrs
Distance: 4 km return
Ascent/Descent: 150 m / 150 m
Conditions: Mostly shady; large rocks on track (wear footwear that gives good ankle support); well trodden but largely unmarked, ok for families with older children; park entry fees apply
More info: Parks and Wildlife Service, www.parks.tas.gov.au

Getting there

Car: Mt Field NP is 75 km northwest of Hobart on the Maydena Rd; drive past the park visitor centre, turn left and continue for about 10 km to a small car park on your right, just after a blue sign: *Mt Field East, Lake Nicholls, Mt Field East Circuit via Windy Moor*

Climbing Heath

Trochocarpa

36 Lake Nicholls

Walk directions

Bauera

1 From the blue sign the track initially leads uphill through open, wet forest comprising mainly younger trees. Moss and lichen covered rocks and boulders line the track and you may find interesting fungi on the damp forest floor. There is also a lot of Bauera, with its pretty nodding flowers, in the understorey.

2 After a few minutes turn right at a Y-junction (the left track leads to the Lake Fenton car park). Take the right branch, which continues uphill at a steady climb, until Mt Field East appears ahead and the track levels off for a while as you pass a wet spot, the drainage out of Beatties Tarn (sadly no longer accessible). There are Tea Tree and Hakeas growing here and bright yellow Sphagnum Moss covers the ground. This moss is harvested in other areas of Tasmania; its moisture-holding and anti-fungal properties make it very useful to plant nurseries.

3 The track curves sharply to the right as you pass Beatties Tarn and remains more or less level past dolerite boulders that increase in size as you progress. On your right you can now catch glimpses of the valley below through the drier open forest. Eventually the track descends slightly to

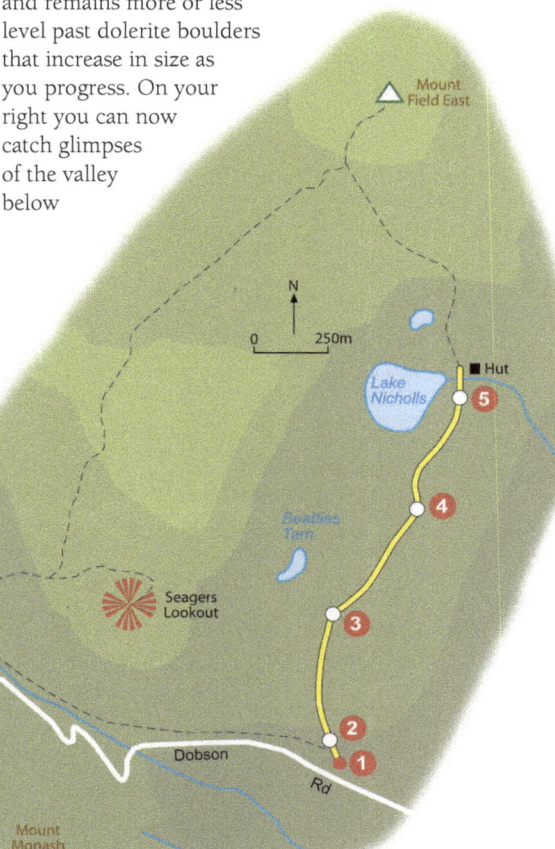

36 Lake Nicholls

a distinct curve to the left by a trio of tree trunks that bear three small orange paint spots.

4 The track now leads uphill to the top of a small glacial moraine which acts as a dam for Lake Nicholls. As you walk along the moraine, the cool, clear waters of the lake can be spotted below on your left. At the far end zig-zag down towards the lake.

5 Hop across the boulders in the outlet stream to reach the shore and hut. Time for a rest and a bite to eat before you return via the same route to your start point.

Native Currant

36 Lake Nicholls

Hobart environment - Mountain Pepper (*Tasmannia lanceolata*)

With its distinctive crimson stems, Mountain Pepper grows in the high rainfall areas of Tasmania and can be up to 5 metres tall. Male and female flowers are borne on separate plants. The fruit is a small, shiny, black berry which was used by indigenous Australians as a medicine and condiment and by early settlers as a pepper and spice replacement. It has found its way back into modern cuisine; leaves or berries, either fresh or dried, are often added to gourmet foods such as cheeses, mustards, dressings, breads and rolls, hamburgers and pates. Mountain pepper is also used by some restaurants to replace the usual black or white pepper to give a 'bushtucker' flavour. But it's as well to use it more sparingly: it's ten times as strong as normal pepper!

37 Historic Richmond

Time appears to have stood still in this historic village. Originally Richmond was settled as the centre of a grain growing area, with a number of wind, water and steam driven mills. Later, it was chosen as the place to bridge the Coal River and quickly became an overnight stopping place for traffic to the East Coast of Tasmania. Construction of the bridge began in 1823 and it is Australia's oldest bridge still in use. A few years later, and before Port Arthur, the gaol, courthouse and barracks were built. However, the village was bypassed in 1872 when the Sorell Causeway was completed and became the preferred route from Hobart to the East Coast. The ensuing reduction in traffic through Richmond stalled further development and caused the village to remain much as it was from that point on. On this amble through history you will find a range of buildings: simple Georgian cottages and grand two storey residences, churches, specialist shops and public buildings. There are also many places to stop for a coffee and a bite to eat.

At a glance

Grade: Easy
Time: 50 mins, but allow much more to do this lovely village justice
Distance: 2½ km circuit
Conditions: Level footpaths, little shade

Getting there

Car: Coming to Richmond from Hobart, continue along Bridge St and turn right into Wellington St; cross the bridge and turn left into the car park in St Johns Circle
Bus: Tiger Line, www.tigerline.com.au, T 6230 8900

37 Historic Richmond

Walk directions

1 From St Johns Circle cross Wellington Street and walk towards the bridge. On your left, just before the bridge, you will pass by Mill House, one of the town's former mills and now a private home. Cross the convict-built, sandstone bridge then veer left and uphill onto Bridge Street. Across the street there are several quaint old cottages, now bed and breakfast accommodation, and the old Richmond Bakehouse dating back to 1830. On the left is Mill Cottage, now the *Peppercorn Gallery*, run by a co-operative of fine local artists and well worth a visit.

2 Next on your left is the village green, where the Village Fair is held annually in autumn – and has been for over 180 years. Further along is the old Court House, now the Post Office and online access centre, and the original Bridge Inn, which operated as a hotel from 1834 to 1975. It is currently occupied by *Sweets and Treats*. A narrow lane leads from here into the Saddlers Court Complex, which is home to a very fine bakery and coffee shop - you may wish to explore this along the way! Continue along Bridge Street and its time-worn flagstones in the front of the *Saddlers Court Gallery* (originally a general store and later a saddlery as the name suggests).

3 Cross Edward Street; the Village Store over the road is still just that and probably one of the oldest general stores still in use in Tasmania. You will soon pass the magnificently

37 Historic Richmond

restored Richmond Arms Hotel. This site originally housed the Lennox Arms Hotel, built in 1827; its old stables are all that remain. The prominent white double storey building further along dates back to 1826. This began its life as a single-storey cottage which was added to in 1830 and then used as a store.

4 Cross Henry Street and, as the road dips downhill, pass a row of three cottages, the first one of which was once the Star and Garter Inn, built in 1830. At the corner of Bridge Street and Blair Street is Oak Lodge (c. 1830), owned by the National Trust and managed by the Coal River Historical Society. This building is open to visitors from 1100 to 1630 daily.

5 Turn left into Blair Street then left again into Bathurst Street. Along here are Rose Cottage (c. 1840s) with its unusually steeply pitched roof, now a private home, and, on the left, the former 'old' Richmond Hotel and staging post for coaches, also now a private residence.

6 Turn right into Henry Street, passing Fernville cottage. When you reach Torrens Street, cast your eye to the right to catch sight of quaint Pop Wright's Cottage. It was built in the 1840s and served as the home for the local butcher and his descendants from 1862 to 1988.

7 On the corner of Torrens and Henry Streets stands the Old Schoolhouse. Built in 1834, this is the oldest State

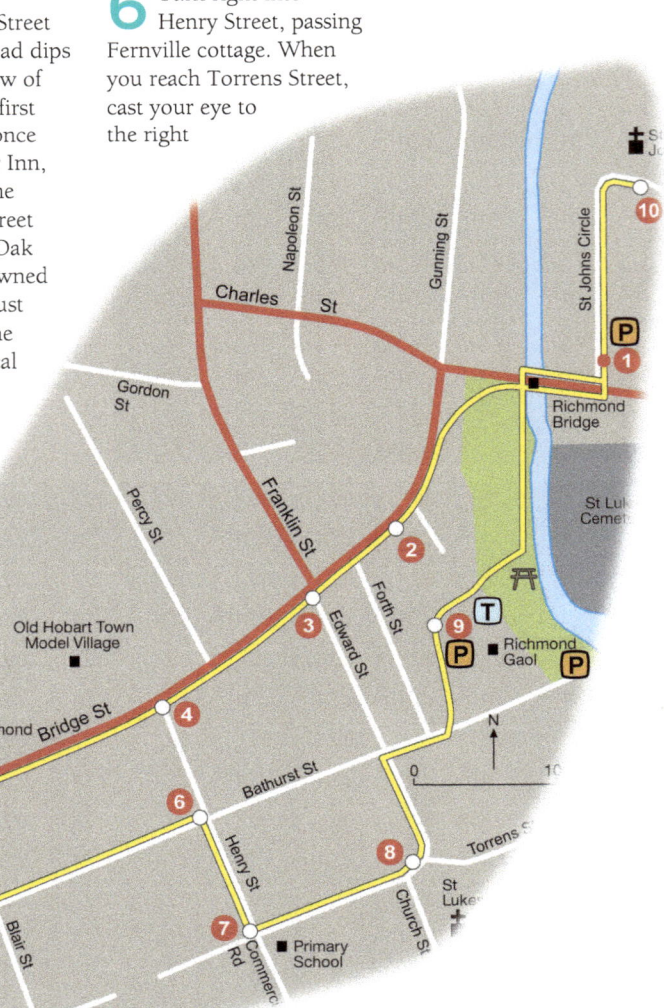

37 Historic Richmond

school in Australia, and is now part of Richmond Primary School. This stone building was designed by the well-known colonial architect John Lee Archer, who also designed St Lukes Church (c. 1834) which you will see on your right as you continue along Torrens Street. Also on the way is the Congregational burial Ground and Emerald Cottage.

8 Turn left into Edward Street, pass The Old Rectory (1831), then turn right into Bathurst Street. As you look ahead towards the Coal River, the prominent Richmond Gaol Building appears on the left. Cross the lawn towards it. This was constructed in 1825 and is well worth a visit; open to the public (with an admission fee) from 0900 to 1700 daily except Christmas Day.

9 Continue past the Gaol and turn right just after the police station to walk through the station car park towards the Coal River. You will find a set of stone steps to take you down to the riverbank where there are picnic areas and a small wooden platform jutting into the river, a favourite spot for weddings. Walk to the bridge and pass under it, then go up the steps to the top and find your way back to your starting point.

10 You can add a short five minute walk up the hill to visit St Johns Roman Catholic Church, the oldest Catholic Church still in use in Australia (it was built in 1837), to complete this historic amble.

Hobart people - John Lee Archer (1791-1852)

Born in Dublin, Archer was appointed Government Architect and civil engineer for Tasmania in 1826 and worked in this capacity for eleven years. During most of this time he designed all government buildings including Richmond Gaol, St Lukes Church and the Old Schoolhouse seen on this walk. His buildings were designed in the Georgian Renaissance style which is plain and solid. In Hobart his extant work includes some buildings in the Anglesea Barracks complex, the Penitentiary Chapel, the Old Parliament House, St Georges Church in Battery Point, and St Johns Church and Orphan School in New Town. These continue to contribute to the character of the city. Later in life Archer became police magistrate at Stanley, in the northwest, where he lived the rest of his life. He is buried in a small graveyard near the Nut at Stanley.

38 Tasman Peninsula excursion – Devils Kitchen to Waterfall Bluff

The Tasman Peninsula was once a bleak and isolated place, chosen by Lieutenant Governor George Arthur to accommodate a penal settlement because it is joined to the Forestier Peninsula to its north by the very narrow Eaglehawk Neck isthmus. Today, coastal areas along the eastern side of the Forestier and Tasman Peninsulas and some southern and western areas of the Tasman Peninsula form the Tasman National Park. This contains some truly stunning coastal scenery, with columnar sea cliffs ranging in height from 100 to 300 metres and spectacular rock formations, including sea-caves, stacks, arches and collapse features, all created by the powerful, pounding wave action of recent millennia. The park is also home to a wide range of animals and plants, some of which are endemic and rare. This walk introduces you to just some of these wonderful features.

At a glance

Grade: Easy/medium
Time: 3¼ hrs return (1½ hrs return to Waterfall Bay)
Distance: 6.7 km
Ascent/Descent: 90 m / 90 m
Conditions: Easy to Waterfall Bay; thereafter track is narrow and steep with unfenced, exposed cliff tops, not suitable for children; both sections are partly shaded
More info: Parks and Wildlife Service, www.parks.tas.gov.au

Getting there

Car: From Hobart, after passing Eaglehawk Neck and Pirates Bay to your left, turn left at the *Blowhole, Tasmans Arch and Devils Kitchen* sign and follow signage to Devils Kitchen

38 Devils Kitchen to Waterfall Bluff

Walk directions

1 The track begins at the *Patersons Arch 1 hr return, Waterfall Bay 2 hrs return* sign at the southern end of the car park and heads straight towards Waterfull Bluff, visible from the start. It leads through coastal scrub containing Banksias, *Allocasuarina monilifera* (a low growing Casuarina), Tea Tree and Swamp Melaleuca (which sports showy, fluffy mauve flowers in spring).

View from Waterfall Bluff

38 Devils Kitchen to Waterfall Bluff

2 From the lookout that appears after about five minutes, you can see the 100 metre high sea cliffs back along the rugged coastline to the north.

3 A further five minutes' walking brings you to another lookout with an interpretive panel that tells about the interactions of life forms in the sea. From here the track begins to climb gradually through wet forest with the dainty pink flowered Baueras, Melaleucas and Banksias in the understorey. There are many other botanical delights to be found here, including Trigger Plants, Ziera and Native Daphne. This area also supports a rich bird life and you may hear cockatoos and honeyeaters overhead.

4 The third lookout is a little further along and looks out over spectacular Patersons Arch.

5 Not much further along, the next viewing platform offers views to the south with Hippolyte Rocks and Cape Hauy in the distance. You will notice tall shrubs such as Native Hop Bush, Blanket Bush and Wild Cherries growing along the track as you make your way to a platform that gives you a particularly good view back along the coast.

6 At the last lookout along this first section of the track is a spectacular view into Waterfall Bay, with the waterfall clearly visible across the small bay, especially after rain. Immediately after, a locked boom gate marks the end of this, easier part of the walk.

7 There are two more lookouts at the Waterfall Bay car park, which is at the end of Waterfall Bay Road. Continue diagonally across the car park towards the *Tasman Coastal Track* sign and enter the narrow bush track which rises steeply into the tall Stringy Bark forest above. You will soon see a walker registration box where you can make a note

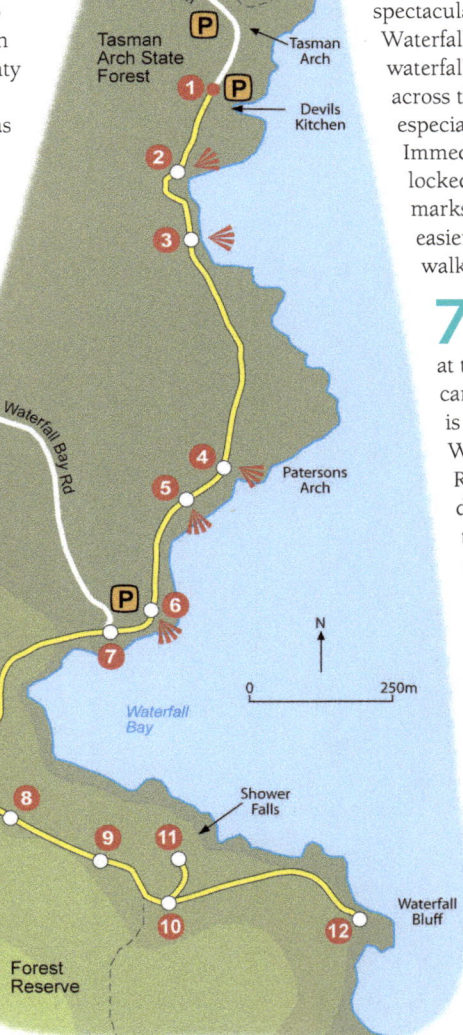

38 Devils Kitchen to Waterfall Bluff

of your setting out on this more challenging section. The track leads up to the top of the cliffs of Waterfall Bay and to the top of the waterfall you saw from the lookout. After about ten minutes of climbing, as the track draws closer to the unfenced cliffs, you will be able to catch glimpses back down to Waterfall Bay.

8 In about fifteen minutes the track begins to dip down slightly and reaches an unfenced rocky area on the left from where (if you don't suffer from fear of heights) you can carefully stare into the incredible abyss!

9 Next a patch of tall Cutting Grass indicates that you are traversing a wet spot where

Out and about - The Blowhole and Cashs Lookout

Both are situated near the start of this walk and are well worth a quick visit.

The **Blowhole** is a 1-kilometre detour from the Tasmans Arch Road and is well signposted. A van in the large car park there sells take-away food and there are public toilets nearby. You can reach the Blowhole and a well-fenced lookout across Fossil Bay via short tracks.

A slightly bigger effort is necessary to climb **Cashs Lookout** to get the birds-eye view that this infamous convict escapee turned bushranger had over Eaglehawk Neck and Pirates Bay. Park in the surfer's car park, which is to your left just after the turn-off from the Arthur Highway into Blowhole Road. Walk up Blowhole Road until you reach the private bitumen drive-way of no 42. Walk up the driveway and turn left into *Cashs Lookout Track* which is signposted and marked with triangular orange markers. Allow about an hour for the return walk.

38 Devils Kitchen to Waterfall Bluff

several small watercourses are heading for the cliff. Camp Falls is not much further: a delightful small waterfall below a small bush camp. A wooden footbridge crosses the creek, above the falls, to a signposted track junction with the *Waterfall Bluff track*. Keep left and follow this along the cliff top.

10 About twenty metres from the wooden sign you will see a fainter footpad leading off to the left along the top of the creek bank. Follow this for a few minutes as it descends down the Manfern-filled watercourse to Shower Falls, which you can actually walk behind.

11 Return to the main track, turn left to continue eastwards and, in only a couple of minutes, you will reach an area from

Shower Falls

Waterfall Bay

38 Devils Kitchen to Waterfall Bluff

where you can see all of Waterfall Bay with Pirates Bay in the background. Then, after a few more minutes, you can catch another stunning view of this iconic coastline (take care to not lose your footing here, particularly in high winds). The track continues in a southerly direction from here.

12 However, this is a good point to turn back and retrace your steps back to Devil's Kitchen. You are bound to notice things along the way that you missed on your way up.

Swamp Melaleuca

Make a day of it

The Tasman Peninsula is one of Tasmania's most visited areas, full of natural and historic features. You may wish to add a few of the following side trips to a day or weekend's excursion.

From the Arthur Highway you can take a left turn at the top of a rise before Eaglehawk Neck, signed **Pirates Beach Lookout**. This is a 4-kilometre long loop road that rejoins the Arthur Highway just before Eaglehawk Neck. You can see 'the Neck' and all of Pirates Beach with Waterfall Bluff and Clemes Peak in the background from the car park at the lookout. The road continues down towards another car park from where a ten minute stroll along a wide gravel path will lead you to the famous **Tesselated Pavement**, a unique rock platform.

A little further along you can park your car and visit the quaint **Officers Quarters Museum** and perhaps take the short walk to the narrowest part of the Neck where a bronze sculpture commemorate the infamous dog line that was installed from shore to shore to prevent convicts from escaping.

As you drive along the Tasmans Arch Road you will pass through '**Doo-Town**', which was originally a holiday shack-town. Each shack was given a name that included the word Doo. There are several amusing names to look out for.

Safety tips

First aid gear

For some of the longer walks, especially when with children, it is wise to carry some basic gear such as a triangular bandage, elastic bandage, band-aids, antiseptic cream, a sachet of salt (to remove leeches), a small amount of vinegar or similar (to treat insect bites) and pain killers, as well as some emergency gear such as a short candle, matches (for lighting fire), whistle, pocket knife, safety pins, a small torch, toilet paper and a foil rescue blanket (available in outdoor shops). Keep it all in a strong, see-through bag for easy access.

Sun and cold

The risk of **sunburn** is high in Tasmania, particularly during daylight saving. Make sure you have sunscreen and wear a broad-brimmed hat from mid morning to mid afternoon to protect yourself.

Hypothermia is a very real risk in Tasmania. It is caused by prolonged exposure to cold, wet and windy conditions without adequate protection and occurs when your body loses heat faster than it can produce it so that core temperature is lowered abnormally as a result. Because it happens gradually and affects your thinking, you may not realize you need help: this makes it especially dangerous. Symptoms can include shivering, slurred speech, lethargy, stumbling, disturbed vision and irrational behaviour. Hypothermia can be simply prevented by being well prepared. Treat by providing shelter, dry clothes and/or body heat from a fit companion. Give warm drinks, chocolate and send for help. Do NOT apply direct heat, massage or give alcohol.

Jack Jumper stings

Jack Jumper ants are very common in Tasmania. They have a one centimetre long black body and orange pincers and legs. They jump at their victim and hold on with their pincers then sting with their tail, much like wasps. They can cause a severe anaphylactic reaction, which can be life-threatening in those susceptible. Symptoms can include a rash, tightening of the throat, swelling of the lips and face and difficulty in breathing. Immediate medical treatment is needed by anyone who reacts thus. If you know you are allergic, consult your doctor who may prescribe Adrenaline/EpiPen as an emergency medication to be carried.

Safety tips

Snakes

The incidence of snake bite is very low in Tasmania and the incidence of death by snake bite is even lower. Although all three Tasmanian snake species are venomous, they tend to slither off as soon as they feel the ground vibrate from your footsteps. If you do manage to surprise one in its favourite sunbaking spot, stand still until it retreats or give it a wide berth.

In the unlikely event that you do get bitten, stay calm and keep still to avoid speeding up your blood circulation. Place some padding over the bite and apply a firm bandage. If possible, immobilise the affected limb by using a splint. Send someone for help or use your mobile phone if you are within range (not always the case in the bush).

Navigation

This guide book or a photocopy of the relevant walk pages will hopefully give you sufficient direction to keep you on track and out of trouble. However, no map is ever 100% accurate and things do change. When following a route with cairns or markers make sure you can see the next one before proceeding, especially in foggy conditions. Some of the walks in this book describe tracks that are indistinct in places and for this reason you are advised to carry a regional **map and a compass** (and know how to use them), particularly for walks in more remote areas.

If you suspect that you are lost, stay on tracks, where you will be easier to locate by anyone looking for you, and do not be tempted to 'bushbash'. Try and call for help on 000 or 112 (the international emergency number). Even if your mobile doesn't have enough signal strength to make a call, try an SMS, which has a better chance of getting through. Give as clear an indication as you can of your position; describe the landscape around you, whether you are on a ridge or in a valley, whether there is water nearby and where the sun is in the sky. Make yourself visible by spreading out anything brightly coloured on the ground or, if possible, lighting an emergency fire with lots of smoke.

Pencil Pine, Lake Dobson

Further reading

Walk into History in southern Tasmania. D. Leaman (1999), Leaman Geophysics, Hobart.

Step into History in Tasmanian reserves. D. Leaman (2001), Leaman Geophysics, Hobart.

A Short History of Tasmania. Lloyd Robson (1997), Oxford University Press.

Secret Tasmania. Philip and Mary Blake (2002), New Holland.

Tasmanian Mammals – a Field Guide. D. Watts (1993), Peregrine Press, Kettering.

The Birds of Australia. Simpson and Day (1984), Claremont, South Yarra.

Guide to Flowers and Plants of Tasmania. Launceston Field Naturalists Club (1981), Reed, Sydney.

An illustrated guide to Tasmanian Native Trees. Kirkpatrick and Backhouse, Mercury-Walch, Moonah.

Tasmanian Streambank Plants. Glazik, Askey-Doran and Black (2004), Rivercare Section, Department of Primary Industries, Water and Environment, Hobart.

Tasmanian Parks and Wildlife Service: www.parks.tas.gov.au.

Needle Bush

Index

1967 fires   133

A-B

Acacia melanoxylon   119
African Boxthorn   89
Alexandra Battery   42-45
Allocasuarina stricta   95
Archer, John Lee   198-199
Arm End   86-89
Atherosperma moschatum   119
Athrotaxis selaginoides   124
Baha'i centre   17
Bandicoot, Eastern Barred   30
Battery Point   16
Beaumaris Zoo site   22
Bedlam Walls   52
Being prepared   5
Bellerive Beach   70
Bellerive Oval   68
Bellerive Wharf   67
Bethune, Walter Angus   65
Bicentennial Park   37-38
Big Bend Trail   145-148
Blackwood   119
Blinking Billy   44
Boronia Beach   93-94
Boronia Beach Walking Track   93-94
Botanical Gardens   18-23
Brown Trout   102
Bruny Island   151-173
Bruny Island history   173
Bush Inn   178
bushwalking groups   1

C-D

Calverts Beach   80
Calverts Lagoon   76-77
Cape Bruny Lighthouse   156
Cape Queen Elizabeth   162-166
Cascade Brewery   35
Cascade Gardens   32-33
Cathedral Rock   140
Celery Top Pine   119

Cenotaph   13, 19
Charles Darwin Trail   70, 72-74
children, walking with   3
Clarence Foreshore Trail   68, 70-71
Cliff top Walking Track   113-114
closures, track   4
Collins Bonnet   145-149
Collins, David   11
Common Wombat   146
compass, use of   207
Conningham Reserve   111-115
Cornelian Bay   24-27
Curtis, Winifred   75
D'Entrecasteaux, Bruni   109
Darwin, Charles   68, 72
Derwent Valley   175-181
Devils Backbone   120-123
Devils Kitchen   200
dogs, walking with   3, 6-9
Doo Town   205
Drooping She-Oak   95
Dunns Creek   128-132

E-F

Eagle Tarn   184
East Cloudy Head   152-155
East West Trail   148-149
Eastern Barred Bandicoot   30
Eastern Shore   52-75
Echidna   154
environment, caring for the   4
EPIRBs   5
Eucalyptus globulus   94
Eucalyptus risdonii   54-55
Eudyptula minor novaehollandiae   166
Exocarpus cupressiformis   171
Fagus   191
Fairy Tarn   188
feet, care for   5
Female Factory   33
Fern Tree   13
Fern Tree Bower Reserve   128-132
Ferntree   47

Index

fires, care with   4
first aid gear   206
fish farms   115
Fishers Hill   54
Fluted Cape   168-172
Fossil Cove   96, 98
fossils   99
French names and the French connection   160-16

G-H

Geilston Bay   52-53
Gellibrand, William and family   87-88
geology around Hobart   99
glacial features   190
Glover, John   31
Goat Bluff   79-80
Gordons Hill   60
Gorringes Beach   83-85
Gorse   89
grades, walking   2
Grass Point   170
Haematopus longirostris   85
Hartz Peak   120-123
Hobart geology   99
Hobart Rivulet   32-34
hop industry   180
Hope (steamship)   79-80
Hunter Island   13
Hunter, Henry   26
hypothermia   206

I-K

Ice houses   138
Jack Jumpers   206
Kaoota to Margate Tramway   107
Kaoota Tramway Track   104-106
Kelly Steps   14
Kermandie Falls   116-119
Kettering   151
King Billy Pine   124
Kingston Beach   92-83
Knocklofty Reserve   28-31

L-N

Labillardiere Peninsula   158-159
Lake Dobson   182-185, 187
Lake Nicholls   192-194
Lake Osborne   124
Lake Webster   188
Lambert Park   37
Lindisfarne Bay   56-58
Little Penguin   166
Location maps   iii-v
Lower Sandy Bay   42-45
Luggaboine   158-159
Lycium ferocissimum   89
M W Simmons Park   56-57
maps, location   iii-v
maps, use of   207
Maritime Museum   16
Mars Bluff   164-165
Miles Beach   164-165
Mountain Pepper   195
Mt Field National Park   182-194
Mt Nelson Signal Station   36-39
Mt Wellington   127-149
Muttonbird   79
Myrtle   119
Narryna Heritage Museum   15
Native Cherry   171
Native Hens   48
navigation   207
Neck, The   167
New Norfolk   176-180
North West Bay river   100-102
Nothofagus cunninghamii   119
Nothofagus gunnii   191

O-P

Officers Quarters Museum   205
Old Schoolhouse   198-199
Pademelons   172
Pandani   185
Pandani Grove Track   182-184, 190
Patersons Arch   202
Phyllocladus aspleniifolius   119

211

Index

Phytophthora cinnamomi 4
Pied Oystercatchers 85
Pinnacle Track 135-136
Pipeline Track 141-142
Pirates Beach Lookout 205
Platypus 103
public transport 2

Q-R

Queen's Domain 18-23
Richea dracophylla 131
Richea pandanifolia 185
Richmond 196-199
Risdon Peppermint 54-55
Rosny 62-71
Rosny Hill Lookout 63-64
Rosny Historic Centre 67
Royal Tasmanian Botanical Gardens 18-23
rubbish, removing 4
Rufous Wallaby 172
Russell Falls 184

S-T

safety 206-207
Salamanca Place 13
Sandy bay 42-45
Sassafas 119
Shag Bay 52-54
Silver Falls 130
snakes 207
Snug 109
Snug Falls 108-109
South Arm Peninsula 76-89
South Bruny National Park 170-172
St Crispins Well 140-143
sunburn 206
Tachyglossus aculeatus 154
Tangara Trail 81-85
Tarn Shelf 186-190
Tasman Bridge disaster 67
Tasman Monument 14
Tasman Peninsula 200-205
Tasman, Abel 14
Tasmania's Floral Emblem 94
Tasmanian Blue Gum 94
Tasmanian Maritime Museum 16
Tasmanian Native Hens 48
Tasmannia lanceolata 195
Telopea truncata 139
Tesselated Pavement 205
The "Mountain" 127-149
Thylogale billardierii 172
timber species 119
Tinderbox Hills 96-97
toileting 5
track closures 4
Truganini 41
Truganini Reserve 38-40
Twighlight Tarn 188-189

U-Z

Ulex europaeus 89
Upper Reservoir 47
Vombatus ursinus 146
Walker, Stephen 13
walking grades 2
walking groups 1
walking times 3
walking with children 3
walking with dogs 3, 6-9
Waratah 139
water, drinking 5
Waterfall Bay 202-204
Waterfall Bluff 205
Waterfront 12-14
Waterworks 46-49
Waterworks 46-49
Waverley Flora Park 72-74
weather 5
Willow Court 179, 180
Wireless Institute 20
Wombat 146
Zig Zag Track 134-139
Zinc Works 54

About the author

Ingrid Roberts is a keen bushwalker and photographer and has explored many wonderful Tasmanian walking tracks during the 50 years she has lived in the state. She has a background in farming and horticulture and has been a member of the Australian Plant Society and is a founding member of the newly opened Tasmanian Bushland Garden on the east coast which showcases the native flora of south-eastern Tasmania. Ingrid has recently completed a BA (Bachelor of Arts) degree with Hon in Geography and Environmental Studies. Through this guide she hopes to inspire the reader to go walking in Tasmania, which is the best way to get to know Australia's beautiful island state and its unique natural and cultural wonders. She is currently working on a walking guide to south-eastern Tasmania.

Acknowledgements

Thanks to all at Woodslane, particularly Andrew Swaffer for his helpfulness, Coral who designed the books and Pablo and his team for the cartography.

Also a special thanks to my partner Graham and members of my extended family, Steffi, Andrew, Emily, Samuel, Heather, Christopher and Emma, who variously gave their time as walk companions, assisted with research and checked walk descriptions (and made cups of coffee when needed!).

Photography in this book

All of the photographs in this book were taken by the author. All photographs are copyright © the author and may not be reproduced without permission.

All of the maps in this book were created by Pablo Candia and his team at A1 Cartography. They are copyright © Woodslane Press and may not be reproduced without permission.

Woodslane Press

Hobart's Best Bush, Coast & City Walks is just one of a growing series of outdoor guides from Sydney publishers Woodslane Press and Boiling Billy. To browse through other titles available from Woodslane, visit www.woodslane.com.au. If your local bookshop does not have stock of a Woodslane or Boiling Billy book, they can easily order it for you. In case of difficulty please contact our customer service team on 02 8445 2300 or info@woodslane.com.au.

Titles include:

Best Bush, Coast and Village Walks of South East Tasmania

$32.99

ISBN: 9781922131195

———————

Australian Geographic Tasmania

$19.99

ISBN: 9781925403923

———————

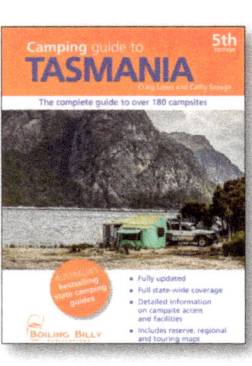

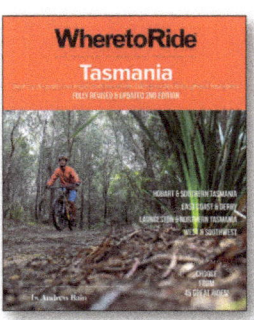

Camping Guide to Tasmania

$32.99

ISBN: 9781921874314

———————

Where to Ride Tasmania

$39.99

ISBN: 9781921874307

Best Walks of the
Great Ocean Road

$24.99

ISBN: 9781922131829

Australian Geographic
Great Ocean Road

$19.99

ISBN: 9781925868050

Australia Free 3

$55.00

ISBN: 9781925403961

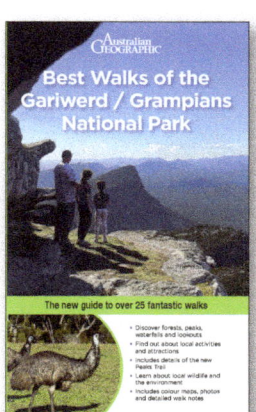

Melbourne's Best
River, Bay and
Lakeside Walks

$32.99

ISBN: 9781921874420

Best Walks of the
Gariwerd-Grampians

$24.99

ISBN: 9781925868159

Best Walks of
Victoria's
High Country

$32.99

ISBN: 9781921874291